PACIFIC COAST HIGHWAY

Including Wine Country of
Napa, Sonoma, Paso Robles

Mike Gerrard and Donna Dailey

www.Pacific-Coast-Highway-Travel.com

PUBLISHED BY
www.Pacific-Coast-Highway-Travel.com

PO Box 2018
Green Valley, AZ 85622
USA

Copyright © 2013 Pacific Coast Highway Travel, Green Valley, Arizona. All rights reserved. No part of this publication may be reproduced, stored in a retrieval system or transmitted in any form or by any means electronic, mechanical, photocopying, recording, scanning or otherwise, except as permitted under Sections 107 or 108 of the 1976 United States Copyright Act, without either the prior written permission of the Publishers.

Introduction

Thanks for choosing our guide to hotels along the Pacific Coast Highway. We can't list every one of the thousands of hotels between San Diego and Seattle, but instead we've chosen a cross-section in different price ranges in or near the main places along the PCH. There are many historic or unusual hotels listed, all of which are likely to make your overnight stay memorable in some way.

We have mostly avoided chains like Motel-6 and Days Inn, of which there are many along the coast. We've nothing against them and have often stayed in them when on the road, but we figure most people can probably find those places for themselves.

City Hotels
In the major cities of Seattle, San Francisco, Los Angeles, and San Diego, there are also far more hotels than we can hope to cover. Instead we provide a few reliable suggestions, in the different price ranges, of those that we think stand out from the crowd.

Price Ranges
Accommodations are listed under three simple headings – Budget, Moderate, and Expensive. We haven't given specific prices, as these can change enormously from season to season. Also, if you visit a hotel website or check on websites like TripAdvisor or Expedia, you might get special deals which turn an Expensive hotel into a Moderate one or a Moderate into a Budget. In addition, some places have a range of rooms and prices that can vary widely. By and large, though, we're reckoning under $100 per room per night is Budget, $100-200 is Moderate, and over $200 is Expensive.

Taxes
In addition to the room rate you can expect to pay tax on top, which varies widely with the region. In California it can be from 10-15% of your bill, adding a hefty mark-up. Oregon has no state-wide sales tax, and local taxes can vary enormously, with local areas able to levy a lodging tax in addition to a state tax. In Washington the statewide sales tax is 6.5% with varying lodging taxes on top, depending on the city or county. In both cases an extra 10-15% on your room bill is a good ball-park figure to allow for.

What's Included
We've called this a guide to hotels to keep it simple, but the book also includes motels, resorts, guesthouses, bed-and-breakfast inns – anywhere you might want to stay while driving PCH.

Private Bathrooms
Unless otherwise stated, all rooms have private bathrooms. Where some of the Budget choices have rooms with shared bathrooms, we say so.

Personal Favorites
We have also designated some hotels that we've particularly enjoyed as our Personal Favorites. They may stand out for their beautiful views, ambience, amenities, fine breakfasts, friendly owners, or other features that make them especially memorable. There's a photo alongside each Personal Favorite, and where there is a longer review on our website we have included a link to it.

Hotel Contact Details
The website, address, and phone numbers are given for each hotel we've listed. If you're planning your trip we assume you'll have internet access and can take a look at the hotel's own website. We've also given the phone number and address in case you don't have an internet connection.

How this Guide is Organized
We've done the main listings in alphabetical order, town by town. We've also put lists of places covered in Washington, Oregon, and California at the front.

Geographical Order
If you want to know which cities and towns are covered in geographical order, excluding the hotels in wine country, then go to the back of the book. Here are maps and North-South lists of places where we have recommendations for each of the three PCH states. We start in Seattle and follow 101 around the Olympic Peninsula, then down the west coast.

Feedback

If you think this book can be improved in any way, or you find any errors then let us know. If rates have changed, or the hotel has changed in some way, let us know. If you have any recommendations for places that ought to be included, or have had a bad experience in any of the hotels listed here, please tell us and we'll update the ebook. You can let us know all these things by email: Mike@Pacific-Coast-Highway-Travel.com

Alphabetical list of places covered

Washington

Aberdeen
Forks
Ilwaco
Long Beach
Olympic National Park
Port Angeles
Port Townsend
Seattle
Seaview
Sequim
Westport

Oregon

Astoria
Bandon
Brookings
Cannon Beach
Coos Bay
Depoe Bay
Florence
Gold Beach
Lincoln City
Newport
North Bend
Port Orford
Rockaway Beach
Seaside
Tillamook
Waldport
Yachats

California
Arcata
Big Sur
Bodega Bay
Cambria
Carlsbad
Carmel-by-the-Sea
Cayucos
Crescent City
Dana Point
Del Mar
Eureka
Ferndale
Fort Bragg
Gualala
Half Moon Bay
Huntington Beach
Laguna Beach
La Jolla
Los Angeles
Mendocino
Monterey
Morro Bay
Newport Beach
Pacific Grove
Pismo Beach
Point Reyes
San Diego
San Diego: Coronado
San Francisco
San Luis Obispo
San Simeon
Santa Barbara
Santa Cruz
Santa Monica
Stinson Beach
Ventura

ABERDEEN, WA
Moderate
A Harbor View Inn
www.aharborview.com
11 W. 11th Street
360/533-7996
877/533-7996
Only four rooms and one suite, and all have good views of Aberdeen's attractive harbor. The house was built in 1905, and while the decor is suitably historic, the facilities are modern, including wi-fi and DVD players. Breakfast is on the sun porch overlooking the harbor, and there's also the use of a guest kitchen.

ARCATA, CA
Budget
Hotel Arcata
www.hotelarcata.com
708 9th Street
707/826-0217
800/344-1221
The Arcata has both Budget and Moderate room rates, from single rooms to two-room suites. It was built in 1915 when the railroad came to town, and later the arrival of U.S. Route 101 boosted its popularity. It's only a simple hotel, nothing fancy as you'd expect from the cost, but it's central, friendly, and the price is definitely right.

ASTORIA, OR
Budget
Astoria Inn Bed and Breakfast
www.astoriainnbb.com
3391 Irving Avenue
503/325-8153
800/718-8153
This cozy Victorian was built in 1890 and has only four rooms, all of them under $100. For this you get treats like cookies and candy, a breakfast that might include Grand Marnier French toast (the owner likes to cook), and all rooms have queen-sized beds. No children or pets.

Crest Motel
www.astoriacrestmotel.com
5366 Leif Erickson Drive
503/425-3141
The Crest is a plain and simple motel, and all but the very best rooms come in at under $100. It looks out over the Columbia River and has a laundry, Jacuzzi, cable TV, and a complimentary breakfast. It's AAA approved, and if you're on a budget it's hard to beat.

Moderate
Benjamin Young Inn
www.benjaminyounginn.com
3652 Duane Street
503/325-6172
800/201-1286
This characterful old inn is on the National Register of Historic Places and has just four large rooms which mix antique furnishings with modern hotel amenities and are priced at $100 or just over. There's a generous gourmet breakfast, too. No pets, no smoking.

Hotel Elliott
www.hotelelliott.com
357 12th Street
503/325-2222
877/378-1924
Both Moderate and Expensive rooms in this very smart downtown hotel, which has a rooftop garden giving lovely views of the Columbia River. There are 21 deluxe rooms and six suites, all non-smoking, with each room having free internet, TV and DVDs, heated bathroom tile floors, and many other amenities.

Expensive
Cannery Pier Hotel
www.cannerypierhotel.com
10 Basin Street
503/325-4996
888/325-4996
This modern luxury hotel in an impressive historic building has great river views from every room. It provides boutique hotel comforts, has its own spa, and complimentary to guests are the breakfast, day-use bicycles, and a nightly wine and lox tasting. The hotel's interior

design has been done by a local artist, Sarah Goodnough, and it reflects Astoria's history and salmon fishing industry in a really stylish way. Some rooms at Moderate prices.

BANDON, OR
Budget
Bandon Beach Motel
www.bandonbeachmotel.com
1090 Portland Avenue SW
541/347-9451
866/945-0133
Only in summer do most room rates go up into the Moderate category, otherwise the Budget rates apply; although, with only 21 motel units, it's best to book ahead. The location is perfect, on a bluff that gives every room an ocean view – the best rooms even have two different ocean views. If you're happy with motel simplicity, then you'll certainly be happy with the Bandon Beach Motel, and the Oregon Island National Wildlife Refuge is right outside.

Moderate
Best Western Inn at Face Rock
www.innatfacerock.com
3225 Beach Loop Drive
541/347-9441
800/638-3092
Given a choice between the various hotel and motel chains, we often opt for a Best Western (and no, we don't get a commission!) They usually have character, and the company is quietly supportive of good causes. The Inn at Face Rock is a great example of the brand, with its pool, spa, hot tub, whirlpool, sauna, steam room, gym, Bandon Bill's Seafood Grill (with live music too), and a proper, complimentary cooked breakfast including biscuits and gravy. Some room rates do get up into the Expensive category.

Expensive
Bandon Dunes Golf Resort
www.bandondunesgolf.com
57744 Round Lake Drive
541/347-4380
888/345-6008
Most people stay here to take advantage of its four golf courses. There are several restaurants and bars, and all the other facilities you'd expect from a large resort-style property. Bandon Dunes has a range of room styles and prices, if you're looking for an overnight stay along this pretty stretch of coast.

BODEGA BAY, CA
Moderate
Bodega Bay Lodge and Spa
www.bodegabaylodge.com
103 Coast Highway One
888/875-2250
This is a Personal Favorite, especially for the views over the wetland and the wildlife that shelters there. Rooms with a west-facing balcony overlooking the marsh are simply magical at sunset. It's a fabulous setting, and the size of the place (84 rooms/suites) means it's small enough to feel intimate but big enough to have facilities like the excellent Duck Club Restaurant, a spa, and an ocean-view pool. There's also access to the beach, and a quiet location a short drive from Bodega Bay itself. You can read a longer review on our website: www.pacific-coast-highway-travel.com/Bodega_Bay_Lodge_and_Spa.html.

Bodega Bay Lodge and Spa

BIG SUR, CA
Moderate
Deetjen's Big Sur Inn
www.deetjens.com
48865 Highway 1
831/667-2377

Deetjens is a piece of Big Sur history, founded by Norwegian Helmuth Deetjen in the 1930s and still retaining that rustic Norway feel. There are 20 cabin rooms, not all of them with private bathrooms, and the facilities are pretty basic. It has tons of character, though, with a fabulous setting in among the redwoods, and you can get a room at a Budget price if you don't mind sharing a bathroom. Other rooms fall into the Expensive category. Deetjen's also has one of the best local restaurants, equally characterful and serving a lot of organic, locally sourced produce. It's on the Pacific Coast Highway, just south of the Henry Miller Library and about three miles south of the Pfieffer Big Sur State Park.

Ragged Point Inn and Resort
www.raggedpointinn.com
19019 Highway One, Ragged Point
805/927-4502

About 50 miles south of the Pfieffer Big Sur State Park and 20 miles north of Hearst Castle, the 30-room Ragged Point Inn stands on its own atop a 350ft cliff and guests have stunning views of that very special Big Sur coastline. You can walk down a cliff path and past waterfalls to get to a private beach, and there's an on-site restaurant and several shops selling work by local craftspeople. Some rooms fall into the Expensive category but mostly they are Moderate. Non-smoking.

Expensive
Glen Oaks Big Sur
www.glenoaksbigsur.com
Highway 1, Glen Oaks, Big Sur
831/667-2105

Just north of Big Sur village and the State Park, Glen Oaks Big Sur is yet another of the delightful places to stay along this stretch of the PCH, with cabins and cottages in the redwoods just back from the road. There's a roadhouse opposite to eat in, if you don't want to drive, although there are plenty of good eating choices around here.

It's nothing fancy, though it has been voted one of the world's most romantic hotels by *Travel+Leisure* magazine, which is high praise indeed..

Post Ranch Inn
www.postranchinn.com
Highway 1, Big Sur
831/667-2200
800/527-2200
This is resort luxury Big Sur style, with rooms built out of redwoods and all the resort amenities you would expect – a superb spa, the award-winning Sierra Mar restaurant, a gym, swimming pools, and free activities like stargazing, cookery demonstrations, yoga classes, whale watching, and many more. You'll find the Post Ranch Inn on the Pacific Coast Highway about 1.5 miles south of the Pfeiffer Big Sur State Park, and half a mile south of the Ventana Inn and Spa.

Ventana Inn and Spa
www.ventanainn.com
Highway 1, Big Sur
831/667-2331
800/628-6500
One mile south of the Pfeiffer Big Sur State Park (that's as close as you get to a street address round here), the Ventana is where the rich and famous go to indulge themselves. It's definitely at the top end of the price range, but if you want to splurge when you're in Big Sur, this is the place to do it. Enjoy the two heated pools, the stunning restaurant food (and wine), the spa, the sauna, fitness facilities, daily yoga and pilates classes, afternoon wine and cheese reception, library, DVD library, daily guided walks... you want it, you got it.

BROOKINGS, OR
Moderate
Portside Suites
www.brookingsportsidesuites.com
16219 Lower Harbor Road
541/469-7100
866/767-8111
As the name suggests, this is right by the port and there are nice ocean or river views from the spacious suites, some of which have their own private hot tubs and all of which are non-smoking. There's

also free high-speed wireless internet in all rooms, and the Blue Water Restaurant and Lounge is on the same grounds. No pets.

South Coast Inn
www.southcoastinn.com
516 Redwood Street
541/469-5557
800/525-9273
There's a range of room options in this 1917 Craftsman-style lodging, including a private cottage in the lovingly tended gardens. You can choose from several rooms, such as the Maybeck Room with its private garden with pond and fountain, the Rose Room with its fantastic ocean views, and the Angel Room, which is the cheapest option. For the quality of accommodation on offer in this AAA-approved property, the room rates are very reasonable indeed.

CAMBRIA, CA
Budget
Bluebird Inn
www.bluebirdmotel.com
1880 Main Street
805/927-4634
800/552-5434
Some room rates are in our Moderate price bracket, but although it's a simple and unpretentious place, it offers excellent value in a good location on Cambria's Main Street, just off the Pacific Coast Highway. It's also on the Santa Rosa Creek, which flows through here and down to the Pacific Ocean, and helps water the lovely gardens through which guests can stroll to unwind from the road trip. Very friendly service.

Moderate
Cambria Pines Lodge
www.cambriapineslodge.com
2905 Burton Drive
805/927-4200
800/445-6868
Some of the lodge's superior rooms and suites are in the Expensive category, but they have more moderately priced rooms, too. There are also 19 rustic cabins set in the lodge's 25 peaceful wooded acres, in the hills on the edge of Cambria village and just off the Pacific Coast

Highway. Facilities include a day spa and a restaurant, which uses organic produce picked from the kitchen garden, and there's music on some nights, too. The Lodge is a Personal Favorite of ours, not least because of its stunning gardens. We spent most of one morning walking round these, taking photos, and it was hard to pull ourselves away. The breakfast was exceptionally good as well. You can find a full-length review of the Lodge on our website: www.pacific-coast-highway-travel.com/Cambria-Lodging.html.

Cambria Pines Lodge

Olallieberry Inn
www.olallieberry.com
2476 Main Street
888/927-3222
805/927-3222
This historic and homely inn is a terrific spot if you want to be in the center of Cambria. It's by the Santa Rosa Creek and is one of the oldest buildings in town, built in 1873. It has won several accolades, and has its own private gardens for guests to relax in. All of the nine rooms have their own bathrooms, and the hosts offer a complimentary afternoon wine tasting with generous hors d'oeuvres, as well as a gourmet breakfast including, of course, a sampling of

olallieberry jam. We arrived after a long drive from Santa Monica and immediately felt at home as we unwound in their colorful gardens with a glass of California wine and some very tasty snacks. Their breakfast is definitely one of the best along the Pacific Coast Highway, making this very much a Personal Favorite. You can read more here and see a slideshow of our photos: www.pacific-coast-highway-travel.com/Cambria_Accommodation.html.

Donna at the Olallieberry Inn

Pelican Inn and Suites
www.pelicansuites.com
6316 Moonstone Beach Drive
805/927-1500
800/222-9160
If the name doesn't charm you then the location across from the beach, the lovely gardens, and the general relaxed atmosphere surely will. Yes, you can see pelicans here, and seals lounging on the beach. Rooms are decorated in a traditional style, very comfortable and spacious, and the room rates (mostly Moderate, some modestly Expensive) include an array of complimentary extras: breakfast, internet, parking, afternoon wine and cheese party, and a huge evening dessert buffet with treats like cheesecake, carrot cake, and chocolate cake. Definitely a Personal Favorite of ours, and you can read more and see more photos on our website: www.pacific-coast-highway-travel.com/Pelican_Cove_Inn_Cambria.html.

In Front of the Pelican Inn and Suites

CANNON BEACH, OR
Moderate
Ecola Creek Lodge
www.cannonbeachlodge.com
208 E. 5th Street
503/436-2776
800/873-2749

Just off U.S. Route 101 at the north side of Cannon Beach, the Ecola Creek Lodge is close to the Ecola State Park, where there are some great hiking trails, wildlife, and beaches. The lodge is in a quiet neighborhood, but is only a few minutes' walk to downtown and its restaurants. It's been in business for almost 60 years and has a kind of New England rustic charm to it. There are 22 rooms and suites, all with wireless internet, and all are uniquely and distinctively decorated using work by local artists and photographers, which is a nice touch. Non-smoking. Pets welcome in some units with advance notice. Some rooms at Budget rates.

McBee Motel Cottages
www.mcbeecottages.com
888 S Hemlock Street
503/436-1392
800/238-4107
The McBee has ten cottages, all attached, though there's a range of sizes and styles – and therefore prices. They were built in 1941 and the owners try to maintain a period feel, without skimping on the modernities. The result is, as they themselves say, "cozy, family lodging." Next to the lobby is the Cannon Beach Café, for all-day Caribbean-style dining.

Expensive
Ocean Lodge
www.theoceanlodge.com
2864 S Pacific Street
503/436-2241
888/777-4047
Right on the beach, the Ocean Lodge was built in the style of a 1940s resort and has every comfort, a very friendly service, a free DVD library, a book library for all the family, a games library, and many other plus points. It's a Personal Favorite for the friendly staff, the free cookies, the decor, and the fact that we were able to hole up in comfort in our room one rainy night and watch a couple of movies from their free library with a bottle of wine. You can relax on the various decks enjoying terrific views of Haystack Rock and the Oregon coast. The Lodge is pet-friendly and 100% non-smoking. See the longer review on our website: www.pacific-coast-highway-travel.com/Ocean_Lodge_Cannon_Beach_Oregon.html.

Ocean Lodge

Stephanie Inn
www.stephanie-inn.com
2740 S Pacific Street
503/436-2221
800/633-3466
There are brilliant views of Haystack Rock and the Oregon coast, and an acclaimed restaurant, in this superb luxury hotel. All rooms have whirlpool baths, HD LCD TVs, DVDs, and one of our favorite features when we're on the road: free internet. Non-smoking, no pets, no children under 13.

CARLSBAD, CA
Expensive
Four Seasons Residence Club San Diego, Aviara
www.fourseasons.com/northsandiego/
7100 Four Seasons Point
760/603-6800
800/332-3442
The Four Seasons is one of the finest resort retreats in California, set in 30 acres and overlooking a lagoon and a wildlife preserve. The hotel organizes wildlife walks and talks, encouraging guests to enjoy and appreciate the location. The facilities are superb, the decor both sumptuous and elegant, and there's a golf course, tennis courts, gym, spa, several on-site restaurants, and lots of family-friendly activities, making it a great base if you're exploring the Pacific Coast with kids.

CARMEL, CA
Moderate
Mission Ranch
www.missionranchcarmel.com
26270 Dolores Street

831/624-6436
800/538-8221
If you're planning a short stay in Carmel, the Mission Ranch has to be one of the accommodation options you consider. It's not just that it's owned by Clint Eastwood, but because it's a relaxing place set in 22 acres and centered on an 1850s farmhouse that has a charm all its own. There are 31 rooms, many with ocean views, and facilities include the six championship-standard tennis courts, a health club, a piano bar with nightly music, a Sunday jazz brunch, a restaurant with great views, and a friendly, intimate atmosphere. The prices are reasonable too, given Carmel's general standards. The rooms in the farmhouse are the least expensive.

Sea View Inn
www.seaviewinncarmel.com
El Camino Real between 11th and 12th
831/624-8778
The Sea View is a characterful Moderate/Expensive option a few minutes' walk from the center of Carmel and close to the beach. The house itself was built at the turn of the century and the owners have tried to keep that historic atmosphere. There are eight rooms, with the two most inexpensive rooms sharing a bathroom. The others all have private baths. There's free wi-fi, but this is definitely a getaway place and there are no TVs or phones in the rooms. Non-smoking, no children under-12.

Expensive
Cypress Inn
www.cypress-inn.com
Lincoln and 7th
831/624-3871
800/443-7443
Renowned for being part-owned by movie legend Doris Day (some of her memorabilia decorates the walls), and for being especially pet-friendly, the Cypress Inn is in the heart of Carmel. This Personal Favorite has 44 extremely comfortable rooms on two floors, a lounge serving meals, and free extras like wi-fi, breakfast, sherry, fresh fruit, and snacks. Pets get even more free treats! Terry's Lounge, devoted to Doris Day's son, the musician and record producer Terry Melcher, is a very popular spot for guests and locals alike. Read more on our

website: www.pacific-coast-highway-travel.com/Carmel_Dog_Friendly_Hotel.html.

Cypress Inn

Lamp Lighter Inn
www.carmellamplighter.com
S.E. Corner of Ocean Avenue & Camino Real (P.O. Box AF)
831/624-7372
888/375-0770
The Lamp Lighter was such a wonderful place that after spending two nights there we wanted to move in permanently. It's a pretty collection of rooms and cottages, very close to both the beach and downtown Carmel's excellent shops and restaurants. It's so pretty, in fact, that several times we saw passers-by stopping to take photos of the white buildings which date back to 1935. Inside, the rooms are spacious and full of light, while outside the patio gardens was where a lot of guests - us included - spent time hanging out and chatting. It's that kind of place, where the guests get to know each other and you feel totally relaxed. We absolutely loved it and this is another of several Personal Favorites we have in lovely Carmel. You can read more about it and see more photos here on our website: www.pacific-coast-highway-travel.com/Carmel-by-the-Sea_Inn.html.

Lamp Lighter Inn

Vagabond's House Inn
www.vagabondshouseinn.com
4th and Dolores
831/624-7738
800/262-1262

We love the name of this place, and we loved our all-too-short stay here. The 13 rooms radiate off a central courtyard lush with waterfalls, plants, and trees, and each room has its own private entrance. Some are done in rustic cabin style, others are a little more grandly decorated, but all have fireplaces, TVs and DVDs, complimentary sherry, tea, and coffee, and the aura of a romantic hideaway, which definitely makes this a great Personal Favorite. Amenities include complimentary wine and cheese each evening, breakfast in your room or in the courtyard, free private car park, free wi-fi – and all in a quiet corner of Carmel but only a short stroll from the center. The reception area is fascinating, with displays from co-owner Denny LeVett's private collections of books, toys and part of his collection of Colt-Patterson guns, which is the largest such collection in the world. Read more and see more photos on our website: www.pacific-coast-highway-travel.com/Vagabonds_House_Inn.html.

Vagabond's House Inn

CAYUCOS, CA
Expensive
Cass House Inn and Restaurant
www.casshouseinn.com
222 N Ocean Avenue, Cayucos
805/995-3669
In the resort of Cayucos to the north of Morro Bay, Cass House is the historic 19th-century home of the ship's captain who founded the town. It has been beautifully and sensitively restored into an inn with five luxurious guestrooms, and has lovely ocean views and relaxing gardens. The room rates also include a full breakfast in the gourmet restaurant which is also open Thursday through Monday evenings.

COOS BAY, OR
Moderate
Coos Bay Manor
www.coosbaymanor.com
955 S 5th Street
541/269-1224
800/269-1224
This Colonial Revival guesthouse is on the National Register of Historic Places and is in a quiet corner of Coos Bay. It has only five rooms plus a family suite, all filled with antiques and a sense of history. There's a friendly welcome and a generous breakfast. Pets and children welcomed.

CRESCENT CITY, CA
Budget
Curly Redwood Lodge
www.curlyredwoodlodge.com
701 Redwood Highway South
707/464-2137
A unique place to stay, opened in 1957 and built from one curly redwood tree (so called because of its curly grain). The motel-style lodge has 36 rooms across from the boat harbor, and while amenities are pretty simple, so too are the prices and it just oozes character. Non-smoking.

DANA POINT, CA
Budget/Moderate
Doubletree Hilton Dana Point
http://doubletree1.hilton.com
34402 Pacific Coast Highway
949/661-1100
Dana Point is where the PCH officially begins, but we'd never actually stayed there. We were glad a local contact recommended the Doubletree Hilton, as it was perfect. It was easy to find, the welcome from the valet parking guy was really warm, and our room was spacious and modern with lovely balcony views towards the ocean. Doheny State Beach is right across the road, and it's a wonderful beach that goes on for miles. The hotel is also only a short and pleasant stroll from Dana Wharf, where the whale-watching cruises go from. Dana Point is especially good for this, and they even have a Festival of Whales here. We'd have no hesitation in recommending

the Doubletree Hilton, if you want a night or two in Dana Point. A Personal Favorite. Read more and see more photos at www.pacific-coast-highway-travel.com/Dana_Point_Hotel.html.

Doubletree Hilton Dana Point

Expensive
Ritz-Carlton Laguna Niguel
www.ritzcarlton.com/en/Properties/LagunaNiguel/Default.htm
1 Ritz-Carlton Drive
949/249-2000
800/240-2000
There can be no finer place to start or end your Pacific Coast Highway drive than the Ritz-Carlton. There are almost 400 rooms and suites here, and every single one of them is spacious and has its own private balcony. The food in the three main restaurants is exceptionally good, and the gardens lead down to white sand beaches. Other facilities include tennis courts, water sports, gym, spa, and plenty of family-friendly activities.

DEL MAR, CA
Expensive
The Grand Del Mar
www.thegranddelmar.com
5300 Grand Del Mar Ct.
858/314-2000
888/314-2030
It's well worth veering inland a little to find this absolutely wonderful hotel set in the Los Penasquitos Canyon Preserve. The views are fantastic, as are the rooms with their soaking tubs, and there are four pools, three restaurants, tennis courts, gym, spa, and a golf course designed by Tom Fazio. If you're not into golf, it doesn't matter – just hike or bike in this inspiring location.

DEPOE BAY, OR
Budget
Trollers Lodge
www.trollerslodge.com
355 SW Route 101
541/765-2287
800/472-9335
Trollers Lodge is the kind of simple, inexpensive place you always hope to find at the end of a day's drive. It has a choice of accommodation styles, with some more expensive rooms if you want to splurge, but its basic rooms are clean and unpretentious, and won't break the bank. It has an oceanfront setting, free wi-fi, cable TV, picnic tables, and a nice peaceful garden setting. Note that not all rooms have ocean views so you'll have to ask if one's available.

EUREKA, CA
Moderate
Carter House Inn
www.carterhouse.com
301 L Street
707/444-8062
800/404-1390
Rates here range from Moderate to Expensive as there are several options, from the conventional but very comfortable Hotel Carter itself to several separate cottages, one of which has three luxury suites. Most of the buildings are modern but done in late Victorian style, and the hotel restaurant, Restaurant 301, is one of the best on

the whole North California coast. It has a wine list that has been rated one of the best in the world, and sources its ingredients from its own cottage garden along the street, and from some of the best local suppliers. Very definitely a Personal Favorite, and you can see more photos and read more about it on our website: www.pacific-coast-highway-travel.com/Eureka_Inns.html.

Carter House Inn

FERNDALE, CA
Moderate
Shaw House
www.shawhouse.com
703 Main Street
707/786-9958

The Shaw House was built in the Gold Rush days of 1854, and has been an inn since 1860. There are eight rooms and suites (two in the Expensive category), and you can reduce room rates by opting for the light breakfast rather than the full cooked gourmet breakfast. You can also book a package to go horseback riding in the Redwoods - the inn isn't far from the Avenue of the Giants.

FLORENCE, OR
Budget
Old Town Inn
www.old-town-inn.com
170 Highway 101
541/997-7131
800/570-8738
The Old Town Inn is easy to find on U.S. Route 101, just north of the Siuslaw River bridge, on the east side of the highway. As the name implies, it's in the Old Town part of Florence, so it makes a good base for an overnight stay with restaurants just a few minutes' walk away. The motel-style property has simple but spotlessly clean rooms, with free wireless internet and cable TV, and a small complimentary 'breakfast-on-the-run.' If your budget is for under $100, this is perfect.

Moderate
Edwin K B&B
www.edwink.com
1155 Bay Street
541/997-8360
800/833-9465
This 1914 Craftsman-style home has six rooms: Winter, Spring, Summer, Autumn, Fall, and Indian Summer. They all have their own bathrooms, with Jacuzzis, and the room rates include complimentary sherry and cookies each evening, and an impressive 5-course gourmet breakfast which, the hosts boast, means you won't need lunch.

Heceta Head Lighthouse
www.hecetalighthouse.com
92072 US-101
541/547-3696
One of the most delightful places to stay along the entire Pacific Coast is this lighthouse turned into a bed-and-breakfast. Owned by the US Forest Service, it serves up gourmet breakfasts and amazing views to those with the foresight to book. Try the 7-course breakfast in the Ona Restaurant and Lounge, which overlooks the Pacific Ocean and the Yachats River. Some rooms in the Expensive category.

FORKS, WA
Budget
Forks Motel
www.forksmotel.com
351 S. Forks Avenue
360/374-6243
800/544-3416
The Forks Motel has 73 units and is just off U.S. Route 101 in the town center. There's a heated pool in summer (when some room rates jump into the Moderate category), and while there's nothing fancy about the place, it's the kind of motel where you know you'll have a good stay at a fair price.

Pacific Inn Motel
www.pacificinnmotel.com
352 S. Forks Avenue
360/374-9400
800/235-7344
Close by the Forks Motel, the Pacific Inn also offers good, basic, affordable rooms in the center of town, with some *Twilight*-themed rooms, too.

Moderate
Manitou Lodge
www.manitoulodge.com
813 Kilmer Road
360/374-6295
A short drive out of Forks and close to the coast, this small bed-and-breakfast is set in ten acres of land and is perfect if you want to have a peaceful Olympic retreat. It claims to be the most westerly bed-and-breakfast in the Lower 48, and it's certainly got a remote feeling, right in the rain forest. Two of the rooms are in a cabin, the rest are in the main lodge. The rates include a good breakfast.

Miller Tree Inn Bed and Beakfast
www.millertreeinn.com
654 E. Division Street
360/374-6806
800/943-6563
The Miller Tree Inn is in a quiet location and was originally built as a farmhouse. It has a handful of rooms and one self-catering

apartment to rent. With an outdoor hot tub (in season), and good breakfasts, this is one of the best places to stay close to Forks.

FORT BRAGG, CA
Moderate
Beachcomber Motel
www.thebeachcombermotel.com
1111 N. Main Street
707/964-2402
800/400-7873
Right on the beach, in summer some of the bigger rooms are Expensive, but out of season there are Budget rates too (just!), if you're prepared to take one of the few rooms that don't have a view. Some rooms have Jacuzzis, hot tubs, and fireplaces; try to get one of the rooms with a private deck.

GOLD BEACH, OR
Moderate
Inn of the Beachcomber
www.innofthebeachcomber.com
29266 Ellensburg Avenue
541/247-6691
888/690-2378
On the ocean side of U.S. Route 101 just south of the center of Gold Beach, the Inn of the Beachcomber is a non-smoking property that covers four acres. There are 48 units and the decor is stylish and unusual, as the rooms are inspired by the Arts and Crafts movement and the beds inspired by Frank Lloyd Wright. In most of the ocean view rooms are chairs based on William Morris designs, while the art work of Georgia O'Keeffe graces the walls. A lovely and unique place to stay, with winter rates for under $100.

Expensive
Tu Tu Tun Lodge
www.tututun.com
96550 North Bank Rogue
541/247-6664
800/864-6357
On the banks of the Rogue River, a few miles inland from Gold Beach itself, but well worth the drive, this is the perfect luxury retreat. Some of the rooms have their own hot tubs, and balconies with

views across the river to the wooded slopes on the far side. We watched an osprey flying by to its nest, and there are bald eagles here too, we were told. There's also a great restaurant (May-October only), and plenty of local activities available for a longer stay, including golfing, fishing, hiking, jet boats, and kayaks. We loved the friendly atmosphere at the early evening reception with complimentary drinks and appetizers. Definitely a Personal Favorite and you can read more on our website: www.pacific-coast-highway-travel.com/Gold_Beach_Oregon_Lodging.html.

At the Tu Tu Tun Lodge

GUALALA, CA
Moderate
Seacliff on the Bluff
www.seacliffmotel.com
39140 Highway 1
707/884-1213
800/400-5053
If your journey brings you to Gualala, about halfway between Mendocino and Bodega Bay, the Seacliff makes a decent, pleasant, and affordable lodging choice. There are 16 rooms, all with private decks and with great ocean views. You can even watch whales from your room at the right time of year. Nothing fancy at all, but very appealing. Non-smoking.

HALF MOON BAY, CA
Moderate/Expensive
Old Thyme Inn
www.oldthymeinn.com
779 Main Street
650/726-1616
800/720-4277

Innkeepers Rick and Kathy run the perfect guesthouse/inn right in the center of the charming little town of Half Moon Bay, a great place for a relaxing stop along the PCH. There are only seven rooms, so individual attention is guaranteed. Some of the rooms fall into our Expensive category depending on the day of the week and time of the year. Rates include one of the best breakfasts you'll find anywhere, and complimentary Californian wine and cheese every afternoon.

Expensive
Seal Cove Inn
www.sealcoveinn.com
221 Cypress Avenue, Moss Beach
800/995-9987
650/728-4114

The Seal Cove Inn is just north of Half Moon Bay in Moss Beach, and we loved it just as much as we enjoy Half Moon Bay itself. There is indeed a Seal Cove a few minutes' walk from the inn, and we loved the chance to stroll down there before we checked out, and to walk along the coast a little way. The inn is in a very quiet location, but directly off the Pacific Coast Highway. Try to get one of the rooms at the back, overlooking the gorgeous gardens, which we also found time to walk in before we left. They were so relaxing. The buffet breakfast was one of the best we've ever had, with a delicious coffee cake, grits, and a bell pepper strata with a red salsa as well as the usual buffet fare. It doesn't have its own restaurant but there's plenty of choice within a short drive. A Personal Favorite, and you can read more and see a photo slideshow here on our website: www.pacific-coast-highway-travel.com/Moss_Beach_Hotel.html.

Seal Cove Inn

HUNTINGTON BEACH, CA
Expensive
Hyatt Regency Huntington Beach Resort and Spa
www.huntingtonbeach.hyatt.com
21500 Pacific Coast Highway
714/698-1234
800/554-9288
All the luxury and facilities you'd expect from a Hyatt Beach Resort and Spa, with over 500 rooms, all with their own patios or balconies, though not all have a full sea view so be sure to ask for one. There are several eating options including The Californian fine dining restaurant, rated Four Diamonds by AAA.

ILWACO, WA
Budget
Heidi's Inn
www.heidisinnmotel.com
126 Spruce Street
360/642-2387
800/576-1032
This is a great budget find, inexpensive but clean and comfortable,

and right on U.S. Route 101 (which is Spruce Street in the center of Ilwaco.) There are 25 rooms plus one dorm room, with both smoking and non-smoking rooms available. Small pets are allowed too, for a modest charge.

LAGUNA BEACH, CA
Expensive
Casa Laguna
www.casalaguna.com
2510 South Coast Highway
949/494-2996
Rooms here fall into both Moderate and Expensive categories, varying with the season and the type of room. Get one at the front and you're looking right over the Pacific Coast Highway – which we did, and we're happy to report very little traffic noise at all. In fact we didn't want to leave our lovely room, but we're glad we did to enjoy the early evening complimentary appetizers with wine, and both of these were definitely a cut above the average. It's a fabulous boutique inn, with lush gardens that have pathways meandering through them, gorgeous rooms, and one of the best gourmet breakfasts we've ever eaten. It's based in what used to be artists' studios,  and it still has an artsy feel. There's free parking and internet, too, a small business center and a delightful two-person spa in one of the rooms. You can read more about this Personal Favorite on our website: www.pacific-coast-highway-travel.com/Laguna_Beach_Inn_and_Spa.html.

Montage Resort
www.montagelagunabeach.com
30801 South Coast Highway
866/271-6953
The Montage makes the most of its coastal location, its buildings spreading out around a hillside that leads down to a cove. It's got a

notable spa, and there are free fitness classes, too. There's a gym, several pools, a choice of restaurants with top-notch cuisine, and lots of kids' activities. The displays by California artists lend the resort a relaxed, artsy feel.

Surf and Sand Resort
www.surfandsandresort.com
1555 South Coast Highway
888/869-7569
The Surf and Sand Resort styles itself after a Mediterranean village, and all of its 167 beach front guest rooms and 13 Laguna Beach Suites have beautiful views of the Pacific. The resort has a fine dining restaurant, lounges and bars, and the Aquaterra Spa. The spa has a wide range of massages and other treatments, as well as offering fitness and yoga training.

LA JOLLA, CA
Expensive
Grande Colonial
www.thegrandcolonial.com
910 Prospect Street
858/454-2181
800/826-1278
This is a real Personal Favorite and definitely one of the best places to stay if you want to be in the heart of La Jolla. It's an easy walk to the beaches and other attractions, and shopping and restaurants are right outside the door – though there is a pool here and the Grande Colonial's own award-winning restaurant, NINE-TEN, is one of the best in southern California. The hotel was built in 1913 and it retains the gracious, old-fashioned air that its name implies, but has every modern comfort, winning it a Four Diamond rating from AAA. We loved it from the moment we arrived and the valet parking guys gave us a really good welcome. The staff couldn't have been more helpful, the whole building just oozes charm and history, and what we appreciated most of all was saying goodbye to our car for two days and exploring everywhere on foot. Read more and see more photos on our website: www.pacific-coast-highway-travel.com/La_Jolla_Luxury_Hotel.html.

Grande Colonial

La Valencia
www.lavalencia.com
1132 Prospect Street
800/451-0772
858/454-0771
La Valencia opened in 1926 and now has a mixture of 112 rooms, suites, and villas at its waterfront location overlooking Scripps Park

and close to several of La Jolla's coves and beaches. It has no fewer than three restaurants, all very different, and an outdoor pool with views of the Pacific Ocean.

Lodge at Torrey Pines
www.lodgetorreypines.com
1148 N Torrey Pines Road
858/453-4420
800/995-4507
Luxury lodge slightly out of La Jolla but in a wonderful location with Pacific Coast views and the coveted Five Diamond rating from AAA. The decor is Arts and Crafts style, very relaxing, and you feel pampered from the moment you arrive. There are walking trails all around, and the Torrey Pines Golf Course is right next door. There's also a pool, gym, spa, and two good restaurants, including the highly acclaimed A.R. Valentien.

LINCOLN CITY, OR
Budget
Palace Inn and Suites
www.thepalaceinn.com
550 SE Highway 101
541/996-9466
866/996-9466
Located right on U.S. Route 101 just north of the crossing over the D River. There are 51 rooms and suites, and although some of the larger rooms are in the Moderate price range in summer, there are some real bargain rates to be found out-of-season. The hotel has a business center, fitness center, sauna, and spa. Room rates include a complimentary breakfast, free wireless internet, and in-room gourmet coffee.

Expensive
Inn at Spanish Head
www.spanishhead.com
4009 S US-101
541/996-2161
800/452-8127
All 120 rooms and suites at this resort have Pacific Ocean views, and there is a range of price options. The inn has its own restaurant, bar, and swimming pool, and you can walk right out and explore the local

beaches. In fact, it claims to be the only resort in Oregon that's built right on the beach.

Salishan Spa and Golf Resort
www.salishan.com
7760 N. US-101
541/764-3600
800/452-2300
A few miles south of Lincoln City in Salishan, this large resort has its own par-71 golf course along with tennis courts, swimming pool, gym, bar, and two restaurants, all in a waterfront setting spread through a wooded hillside. One of the most luxurious places along the Oregon coast.

LONG BEACH, WA
Budget
Anchorage Cottages
www.theanchoragecottages.com
2209 Boulevard North
360/642-2351
800/646-2351
A few blocks off U.S. Route 101 and one mile north of the center of Long Beach, the Anchorage Cottages have rooms in both the Budget and Moderate categories. There are ten cottages to rent, some with one bedroom and some with two. All are really cozy, with gardens around them and in a quiet location. Walk down the path through sand dunes to reach 28 miles of beaches. The cottages all have good kitchens so you can self-cater on a longer stay, though there are plenty of restaurants nearby. You can also use the BBQ equipment onsite.

Moderate
Moby Dick Hotel, Restaurant and Oyster Farm
www.mobydickhotel.com
25814 Sandridge Road, Nahcotta
360/665-4543
800/673-6145
The Moby Dick is a quirky characterful place, with a yurt in the grounds that people can use for retreats, and a bohemian atmosphere that it's had since it opened in 1930. It has ten guest rooms, all individually and attractively decorated, and some are available at

Budget rates though these don't have private bathrooms. It also has its own restaurant and oyster farm.

LOS ANGELES, CA
Moderate
Figueroa Hotel
www.figueroahotel.com
939 S. Figueroa Street
213/627-8971
800/421-9092
Good choice for a slightly less expensive downtown option, this 1926 Spanish-style building has 287 rooms and suites, its own restaurant and bars, and a pool too, great for relaxing after a day's LA sightseeing. You also get movie stars and musicians hanging out here after concerts.

Kawada Hotel
www.kawadahotel.com
200 South Hill Street
213/621-4455
800/752-9232
This is about as cheap as it gets in downtown LA, and perfect if you don't mind it simple and basic. There are 116 rooms and all have TVs and high-speed internet. There are also studios at even cheaper rates if you want a base for a longer stay.

Expensive
Beverly Hills Hotel
www.beverlyhillshotel.com
9641 Sunset Boulevard
310/276-2251
800/283-8885
The ultimate luxury 5-star Hollywood hotel, used by stars, agents, directors, politicians, royalty – you name it. You may or may not see them, though, as they prefer to use the private bungalows, but non-celebrity guests still get the star treatment. Facilities include several bars and restaurants, tennis courts, gym, spa, and the pool where everyone hangs out.

Farmer's Daughter Hotel
www.farmersdaughterhotel.com
115 S. Fairfax Avenue
323/937-3930
800/334-1658
On the Beverly Hills edge of Hollywood and not far from the CBS Studios (though you'll see studio audiences staying here, not the stars), the Farmer's Daughter has 66 non-smoking guestrooms that have been given a boutique makeover, and its own pool. It's on the Moderate side of Expensive, and good value for its location.

Millennium Biltmore Hotel
www.millenniumhotels.com
506 S. Grand Avenue
213/624-1011
866/866-8086
The Biltmore is one of the best addresses if you want or need to be in downtown LA. It has almost 700 rooms and suites and a glitzy reputation - you may recognize its stately facade and sumptuous public rooms as it's appeared in numerous films. There are three restaurants, several bars, a Roman-style indoor pool, and a gym.

MENDOCINO, CA
Expensive
MacCallum House
www.maccallumhouse.com
45020 Albion Street
707/937-0289
800/609.0492
Guests here enjoy one of the best locations and one of the best properties that is actually in Mendocino itself. Six rooms are in the main house, and have soaking tubs and sleigh beds, while there are also some separate suites, vacation rentals, and a separate property: the Mendocino Village Inn. All are kept to the same high standard, and many rooms have breathtaking views of the dramatic Mendocino coast.

Stanford Inn by the Sea
www.stanfordinn.com
Coast Highway and Comptche Ukiah Road
707/937 5615
800/331 8884
This is one of the most eco-friendly resort hotels along the California coast, and its Four Diamond rating from AAA show just how comfortable it is, too. All the rooms are really spacious with wood-panelled walls, ocean views, comfy feather beds, and wood-burning stoves. The atmosphere is rustic but luxurious, and the on-site Ravens restaurant, which is vegan, produces some of the best food you'll find for miles around. The public areas are also very spacious and relaxing, and there's a lovely swimming pool, and gorgeous gardens to walk around (and which also supply the restaurant). This is a great Personal Favorite and a place we can't wait to go back to. You can read why and see a few more photos on our website: www.pacific-coast-highway-travel.com/Stanford_Inn_by_the_Sea_Mendocino.html.

Stanford Inn by the Sea

MONTEREY, CA
Moderate
Mariposa Inn and Suites
http://mariposamonterey.com
1386 Munras Ave
831/649-1414
800/824-2295
This was a real find for us, just off the Pacific Coast Highway and a really bright and friendly place, although it doesn't look like much from the outside. Our room had a huge balcony with a table, umbrella, and four chairs, and inside it was very spacious and modern. We loved the colorful photos and paintings of sea creatures, the funky furniture designs, and the easy-to-light fire in the corner. There's free, private covered parking, and it's very easy to find. The one drawback is that it's a bit of a way out of the centre, but if you're arriving late or leaving early, it's worth that small sacrifice to be able to zip right off or onto the highway. Another Personal Favorite, with a longer review and more photos on our website: www.pacific-coast-highway-travel.com/Monterey-Inn.html.

Mariposa Inn and Suites

Monterey Bay Lodge
www.montereybaylodge.com
55 Camino Aguajito
831/372-8057
800/558-1900
This small but popular garden hotel has 46 rooms including two family rooms and a one-bedroom suite, and is well equipped with an outdoor pool, spa, restaurant, free wi-fi and parking. It's close to the beach and the old part of town, and you can walk to Fisherman's Wharf which is about half a mile or so away. The rooms are simply decorated and they're bright and clean, while the garden courtyard makes it a relaxing place to stay. Some rooms are Budget, especially with their AAA discount.

Monterey Hotel
www.montereyhotel.com
406 Alvarado
831/375-3184
800/966-6490
Located in downtown Monterey not far from Fisherman's Wharf, the hotel offers special packages which include tickets to the fabulous Monterey Bay Aquarium. The hotel first opened in 1904, and the historic building has no elevators and maintains its original European style. The 45 rooms and suites have handmade furniture, marble baths, and plantation windows for a Colonial feel.

Hotel Pacific
www.hotelpacific.com
300 Pacific Street
831/373-5700
800/554-5542
We stayed at this chic boutique Monterey hotel recently and you couldn't have a better location, less than a 5-minute walk to Fisherman's Wharf. It's even closer to the museums of the Monterey State Historic Park, and maybe a leisurely 30-minute walk along the Monterey Peninsula Recreational Trail to the Monterey Bay Aquarium. It has a large underground private car park, for which there's a daily fee but this is a boon in downtown Monterey. All the rooms have fireplaces and very comfy feather beds, and they all have either a patio or a balcony. The rooms are in several Colonial-style buildings, with hidden courtyards and lots of flowers around, and

sculptures and paintings decorate the light and spacious breakfast room - it was a good breakfast too! A Personal Favourite of ours, you can read a full-length review on our website: www.pacific-coast-highway-travel.com/Monterey-Boutique-Hotel.html.

Hotel Pacific

Expensive
The Old Monterey Inn
www.oldmontereyinn.com
500 Martin Street
831/375-8284
800/350-2344
One of the nicest places in Monterey, close to downtown yet surrounded by its own beautiful gardens. The historic building was once the home of Monterey's first mayor but is now run as a boutique bed-and-breakfast inn, with a Four Diamond rating from AAA and many other awards and accolades. The decor and furnishings retain the historic feel, but the rooms are luxuriously appointed, some with fireplaces, private entrances, skylights, and stained-glass windows. There's also a small spa. It's not cheap, but certainly worth it.

MORRO BAY, CA
Moderate
The Inn at Morro Bay
www.innatmorrobay.com
60 State Park Road
805/772-5651
800/321-9566

Near the ocean and actually located inside Morro Bay State Park, the Inn couldn't have a better location if you want to enjoy Morro Bay's wildlife and seashore as it's set in a 4,000-acre estate. There are 97 rooms and one cottage at a range of prices from Budget to Expensive. Facilities include an exceptional restaurant and spa treatments, while the Morro Bay Golf Course is right next to the hotel. It was easy to find (exit onto main Street and keep going till you enter the Park), and we loved being able to walk out in the morning and enjoy the seashore, while watching the hundreds of birds which nest nearby. A terrific and filling breakfast too. The hotel was being renovated while we were there, but that's now been done. We really enjoyed our short stay here, which is why we've made it a Personal Favorite. Read a longer review on our website: www.pacific-coast-highway-travel.com/Inn-at-Morro-Bay.html.

The Inn at Morro Bay

NEWPORT, OR
Moderate
Newport Belle Bed and Breakfast
www.newportbelle.com
Dock H, Newport/South Beach Marina
541/867-6290
800/348-1922
The only riverboat bed-and-breakfast in America, the Newport Belle is moored in the marina and easy to find as it's located where U.S. Route 101 crosses Yaquina Bay. There are five staterooms available, each with its own bathroom, and room rates include breakfast and wine, soft drinks, and snacks in the evening. There are no pets and no children allowed on board, and the Newport Belle is closed from November through mid-February.

Sylvia Beach Hotel
www.sylviabeachhotel.com
267 NW Cliff Street, Nye Beach
541/265-5428
888/795-8422
Sylvia Beach founded the Shakespeare and Co. bookshop in Paris, and each of the rooms in this unique and quirky hotel is named after and designed for a particular author. You may not want the Poe Room for a romantic honeymoon, but there are plenty of others to choose from, including J.K. Rowling, Mark Twain, Amy Tan, Jules Verne, and John Steinbeck. Atmosphere takes precedence over modern hotel amenities, but it's a great place to stay. Room rates vary with the season and days of the week, as well as the room, so some are Budget at certain times, but mostly expect to pay Moderate prices.

The Whaler Motel
www.whalernewport.com
155 SW Elizabeth
541/265-9261
800/433-9444
The Whaler looks out at the Pacific, a few blocks off U.S. Route 101 and not far from Yaquina Bay and the Newport bayfront. All 73 rooms have their own balcony and an ocean view, and there are also four houses to rent, also with ocean views. Rooms have easy beach access. The motel has its own heated indoor pool and spa, and as well as breakfast the room rates include a hot beverage bar till 10pm.

NEWPORT BEACH, CA
Expensive
The Island Hotel
www.islandhotel.com
690 Newport Center Drive
949/759-0808
866/554-4620
If you want to combine California comfort and shopping, this is a good base as it's next to the huge Fashion Island shopping center. The spa here is also especially good and has nine treatment rooms, and there's tennis, swimming pool, gym, the Palm Terrace Restaurant, and the Palm Terrace Lounge. Golfers have access to the Pelican Hill Golf Club which has two oceanfront courses by Tom Fazio.

NORTH BEND, OR
Moderate
Mill Casino Hotel and RV Park
www.themillcasino.com
3201 Tremont Avenue
541/756-8800
800/953-4800
Native-American owned, the Mill Casino Hotel is right on the Pacific Coast Highway and lots of the rooms have great views over the Coos Bay waterfront. The presence of the casino (which isn't intrusive if you're not into gaming) means there's good and inexpensive food, with a choice of eating and drinking places. There's an RV Park alongside too. Try to book a room in the new hotel tower for the best views of all. We were lucky enough to get one of these, a vast suite whose bathroom was bigger than most hotel rooms. You could lie in the Jacuzzi tub and watch the sunset over the bay. On our own most recent Pacific Coast Highway trip this hotel proved to be one of the unexpected delights and instantly became a Personal Favorite. Read and see more here: www.pacific-coast-highway-travel.com/North_Bend_Casino_Hotel.html.

Mill Casino Hotel and RV Park

OLYMPIC NATIONAL PARK, WA
Moderate
Kalaloch Lodge
www.thekalalochlodge.com
157151 US-101
360/962-2271
866/525-2562
Kalaloch Lodge is right by the sea and has several types of rooms and cabins available, with its own exceptionally good restaurant and a shop selling provisions. The main lodge building, where the restaurant is located, has several rooms and suites with ocean views. Other accommodation is in cabins spread around the site, with the Bluff Cabins having ocean views and the Log Cabins set back a little so lacking the full views. The accommodation is simple, and in keeping with the surroundings, so don't expect plush luxury but do expect a historic place with great charm and character. A Personal Favorite and you can read about this and other Olympic National Park accommodation on our website: www.pacific-coast-highway-travel.com/Olympic_National_Park_Accommodation.html.

Kalaloch Lodge

Lake Crescent Lodge
www.olympicnationalparks.com/accommodations/lake-crescent-resort.aspx
416 Lake Cresent Road
360/928-3211
The Lake Crescent Lodge is right by the lake, a wonderful setting. The various rooms and cabins range in style and price, so check the website for the different options. There's an excellent on-site restaurant too, but only in summer.

Lake Quinault Lodge
www.olympicnationalparks.com/accommodations/lake-quinault-lodge.aspx
South Shore Road, Lake Quinault
360/288-2900
800/562-6672
This lodge was built in 1926 and has a superb location right on Lake Quinault with walking trails all around, and a highly regarded restaurant too. This is the Roosevelt dining room, named after President Franklin D. Roosevelt who visited the Lodge in 1937 and who was inspired to declare the whole area a National Park. The accommodation options vary in style and quality, and therefore price too, so if booking ahead be sure to check that you're getting the kind of room that you want. Rooms in the lodge are more comfortable, while the boathouse rooms have more of a basic hostel-style feel to them, but either way it's hard to beat this spot. A Personal Favorite

and you can read about this and other Olympic National Park accommodation on our website: www.pacific-coast-highway-travel.com/Olympic_National_Park_Accommodation.html.

View from Lake Quinault Lodge

Rain Forest Resort Village
www.rainforestresort.com
516 S. Shore Road, Lake Quinault
360/288-2535
800/562-0948
Right by the lake, the resort has its own restaurant and laundry, rooms have TVs and some even have Jacuzzis, all very welcome after a day hiking and exploring the surrounding Olympic National Forest.

Sol Duc Hot Springs Resort
www.olympicnationalparks.com/accommodations/sol-duc-hot-springs-resort.aspx
12076 Sol Duc Hot Springs Road
866/476-5382
No prizes for guessing that this is a resort which has hot water springs. There's also a hot water swimming pool and plenty of hiking around. The rooms are basic, but that's reflected in the price, and the facilities include a restaurant and a provisions store.

PACIFIC GROVE, CA
Moderate
Andril Fireplace Cottages
www.andrilcottages.com
569 Asilomar Boulevard
831/375-0994

In high season prices spill over into the Expensive category, but this family-owned cottage-style motel offers good value for money across from the Asilomar State Park. The rooms aren't fancy, but they all have good kitchens, private decks, free wi-fi, wood-burning fireplaces (with free wood), and there's an outdoor Jacuzzi and barbecue, too.

Expensive
Green Gables Inn
www.greengablesinnpg.com
301 Ocean View Boulevard
831/375-2095
800/722-1774

This inn was built in 1888 and has been restored without losing its historic charm... and without losing its fantastic views over Monterey Bay. There are 11 rooms, three of which share a bathroom, and all have a complimentary breakfast, newspaper, afternoon wine and hors d'oeuvres, homemade cookies, and many other free extras. Some are in the Moderate price range.

The Seven Gables Inn
http://thesevengablesinn.com
555 Ocean View Boulevard
831/372-4341

The Seven Gables works in tandem with the adjacent Grand View and they do indeed provide magnificent vistas over Monterey Bay from rooms that spread across several buildings.

PISMO BEACH, CA
Budget
Shell Beach Inn
www.shellbeachinn.com
653 Shell Beach Road
805/773-4373
800/549-4727

This 10-room inn still shows its origins as a motel, but it's a comfortable, convenient, and inexpensive place to stay on the road that leads to the beach, though it does have its own small swimming pool if you're feeling lazy. There are no other guest facilities, but everything you want is within walking distance.

Expensive
Dolphin Bay Resort and Spa
www.thedolphinbay.com
2727 Shell Beach Road
805/773-4300
800/516-0112
Luxury resort with 62 spacious one- and two-bedroom suites overlooking Shell Beach, which is just a short walk away. The resort also has its own infinity pool, gym, and highly-rated day spa and restaurant.

POINT REYES, CA
Expensive
Nick's Cove
www.nickscove.com
23240 Highway 1, Marshall
415/663-1033
On Tomales Bay, north of the turn-off to the Point Reyes National Seashore, Nick's Cove is one of the best places to stay to enjoy this area. There are five waterfront cottages and seven water-view cottages, all of them done out in a kind of rustic-chic style. The acclaimed restaurant serves organic produce from Scottish salmon to the local clams and oysters.

PORT ANGELES, WA
Budget
The Downtown Hotel
www.portangelesdowntownhotel.com
101½ E. Front Street
360/565-1125
866/688-8600
A simple name for a plain and simple hotel, but it's clean and comfortable, close to the ferry, and the prices are hard to beat. Some rooms share a bathroom, others have private baths, and these stray over into the Moderate price bracket in summer.

Moderate
Colette's Bed and Breakfast
www.colettes.com
339 Finn Hall Road
360/457-9197
877/457-9777
Colette's is a wonderful retreat set in 10 acres of land right beside the Strait of Juan de Fuca and 10 miles east of Port Angeles itself. All five suites also overlook the water, and have all the luxuries including two-person Jacuzzis. The owners also include all kinds of treats in the room price, such as the exceptional breakfasts, wine tastings, and night-time chocolates.

Five SeaSuns Bed and Breakfast
www.seasuns.com
1006 S. Lincoln Street
360/452-8248
800/708-0777
Beautiful gardens and views are just two of the reasons for staying here, in one of the bed-and-breakfast's five rooms which are named – and decorated - for the four seasons plus an Indian summer.

PORT ORFORD, OR
Moderate
Floras Lake House by the Sea
www.floraslake.com
92870 Boice Cope Road
541/348-2573
Floras Lake is a freshwater lake on the far side of a sand spur from the Pacific. This bed-and-breakfast with only four rooms has a sauna right by the lake, and a windsurfing school, too. The rooms all have private baths/showers, but no TVs. Open from mid-February to mid-October.

PORT TOWNSEND, WA
Budget
Palace Hotel
www.palacehotelpt.com
1004 Water Street
360/385-0773
800/962-0741

Set in one of the town's historic buildings, the hotel dates from 1889 and was at one time a bordello. The 19 rooms are named after various ladies of the night, and although it's basic, the rooms are large. It's fun and inexpensive, offering Budget rooms as well as some in the Moderate price range.

Moderate
Ann Starrett Mansion
www.starrettmansion.com
744 Clay Street
360/385-3205
800/321-0644
If you're at all interested in history, then you'll love staying in this 1889 mansion with its turret and the period furniture in its eight guest rooms and suites. You feel privileged to be staying in one of the town's more interesting buildings, now a nicely-run boutique hotel.

Manresa Castle
www.manresacastle.com
7th and Sheridan Streets
360/385-5750
800/732-1281
If you like a hotel with character, then this 1892 mansion certainly provides it, combining historic atmosphere with basic modern facilities. It has its own restaurant and is very central, but if you're staying in summer note that the rooms have no air conditioning. Perhaps the free wi-fi might make up for that.

Expensive
Tides Inn
www.tides-inn.com
1807 Water Street
360/385-0595
800/822-8696
This 43-room hotel has a beachfront location next to the ferries, so it can get busy in summer, especially as it has some Moderate rooms alongside the slightly pricier rooms and suites. Several rooms have decks with private Jacuzzis. Non-smoking. No pets.

ROCKAWAY BEACH, OR
Budget
Trade Winds Motel
www.tradewinds-motel.com
523 N. Pacific Street
503/355-2112
800/824-0938
Just off U.S. Route 101 and 50 feet from the beach, the Trade Winds Motel has a wonderful location. You can even watch migrating whales from the balconies of the rooms here. Prices in the 19 rooms range from Budget to Moderate, depending on the time of year and type of room,. Some pet-friendly units are available.

SAN DIEGO, CA
Budget
500 West Hotel
http://500-west-san-diego.hotel-rv.com
500 W Broadway
619/234-5252
Close to the Amtrak station and a few blocks back from the waterfront, the 500 West provides inexpensive accommodation that's also close enough to the downtown/Gaslamp Quarter attractions. With rooms well under $100 a night, this is a cross between a hotel and a hostel, housed in a historic 1920s landmark building. Rooms share bathrooms but all have TVs and wireless internet.

La Pensione
www.lapensionehotel.com
606 West Date Street
800/232-4683
619/236-8000
There aren't too many boutique hotels at budget prices but La Pensione is one of them. With a downtown location in Little Italy, only a few blocks from I-5, it's a great bargain choice to start or end your PCH drive. There are 68 rooms and they range from the Budget standard rooms to the more expensive suites, but all have private bathrooms. There's also a café and a restaurant onsite, and free wireless internet for all guests.

Moderate
Gaslamp Plaza Suites
www.gaslampplaza.com
520 E. Street
619/232-9500
800/874-8770
In the heart of the Gaslamp district, a great place to be for restaurants and nightlife, you'll find this characterful hotel that was built in 1913. It has 64 rooms and suites, its own restaurant and bar, and a rooftop terrace where you can enjoy the complimentary breakfast. It isn't fancy but it's good, inexpensive central accommodation (which means you usually need to book ahead).

Expensive
Britt Scripps Inn
www.brittscripps.com
406 Maple Street
619/230-1991
888/881-1991
The Britt Scripps Inn is a truly luxurious accommodation option, on Bankers Hill in a beautiful Victorian building. It has just nine guest bedrooms, filled with period antiques but also the latest in modern comforts like flat-screen LCD TVs and high-speed internet. Room rates also include a full breakfast and an evening wine and cheese tasting.

Sheraton San Diego Hotel & Marina
www.starwoodhotels.com
1380 Harbor Island Drive
619/291-2900
Five restaurants, three pools, its own spa and fitness center, and a great location right on San Diego Bay are just some of the things that mark this hotel out as one of the better places to stay if you prefer resort-style accommodation rather than a city center hotel. The center of San Diego is only about three miles away, and the Sheraton is also very close to the international airport, if you have early or late flights to take into account.

US Grant
www.usgrant.net
326 Broadway
619/232-3121
800/237-5029
This is a downtown landmark, on the National Register of Historic Sites, and a luxury hotel that's also part of San Diego's history. It has 223 guest rooms and another 47 suites. There are chandeliers and marble floors, and original artworks in the rooms, which have been modernized without losing their opulence. The classic art-deco Grant Grill restaurant is an excellent place to eat even if you're not staying at the hotel.

Westin Gaslamp Quarter
www.westingaslamp.com
910 Broadway Circle
619/239-2200
800/937-8461
The Gaslamp Quarter of San Diego is a great place to be if you want to make the most of the city's restaurants, bars, shopping, and nightlife. The Westin has some very reasonably priced rooms for its location, though others are in the Expensive category. It has an outdoor pool, Pure Body Spa, fitness center, restaurant, and bar.

SAN DIEGO: CORONADO, CA
Expensive
Coronado Island Marriott Resort and Spa
www.marriotthotels.com/sandci
2000 2nd Street
619/435-3000
800/543-4300
This resort has all the amenities you'd expect – restaurant, bar, pools, tennis, beach and water sports, gym, and spa. The 16 acres of grounds on the waterfront are lovely and lush and the rooms are, well, very roomy.

Hotel del Coronado
www.hoteldel.com
1500 Orange Avenue
619/435-6611
800/468-3533

This big and busy resort opened in 1888 and today it's a tourist attraction as well as *the* place to stay in Coronado. Some rooms are still in the original building, which are great if you want the historic atmosphere, but there are also more modern rooms in separate newer buildings, and these are closer to the private beach and all its watersports options.

SAN FRANCISCO, CA
Budget
San Remo Hotel
www.sanremohotel.com
2237 Mason Street
415/776-8688
800/352-7366

This is a very basic but fun budget choice, and though rooms have no phones, TVs or private bathrooms (here a sink is a luxury), it is just a few blocks from Fisherman's Wharf. Apart from the lack of the usual amenities, the 62 rooms are really comfortable and nicely decorated. So if you don't mind the basics, at under $100 for a city center choice, the San Remo is hard to beat.

Moderate
Beresford Arms
www.beresford.com/arms/default.htm
701 Post Street
415/673-2600
800/533-6533

A few blocks from Union Square, the Beresford Arms is a less-expensive hotel based in a Victorian building which is on the National Register of Historic Places. There are 95 guest rooms and suites, with all the suites having whirlpool baths as well as either kitchens or wet bars. Some rooms are even in the Budget range, while others are in the Expensive. There's also a sister hotel, the Hotel Beresford, at 635 Sutter Street, about a block away.

The Mosser
www.themosser.com
54 4th Street
800/227-3804
415/986-4400
How many hotels have their own recording studio? That's the kind of place the Mosser is, and the reason is that it was owned by Charles W. Mosser, a singer and songwriter who was rather more successful as a property developer. The result is a hotel with a character all its own, combining contemporary decor with the historical feel of a building that dates from 1913. It's got a central location, close to the Museum of Modern Art, but there is only valet parking available which adds to the cost. Note that the Mosser has 54 Budget-price rooms with shared bathrooms as well as its 112 deluxe rooms which have private bathrooms. All are non-smoking.

Expensive
Mandarin Oriental
www.mandarinoriental.com/sanfrancisco
222 Sansome Street
415/276-9600
800/622-0404
Easily one of the best hotels in town, located in the Financial District and with fabulous views of the city, the Bay, the Bay bridges, and even the Golden Gate Bridge. Silks Restaurant is another of its highlights, and there's a fitness center, too. If you don't mind paying for something special, this is the place.

San Francisco Marriott Marquis
www.marriott.com/hotels/travel/sfodt-san-francisco-marriott-marquis/
55 Fourth Street
415/896-1600
888/575-8934
We stayed here when we had a few days in San Francisco recently, and it was a great location and an impressive hotel. We loved being able to walk to lots of the attractions, while the various drinking and dining options were first class - don't miss the aptly-named The View Restaurant and bar on the hotel's 39th floor. There are 1,362 rooms and another 137 suites. Try to get one with a city view.

Taj Campton Place
www.tajhotels.com
340 Stockton Street
415/781-5555
866/332-1670

If you want to be downtown near Union Square there are lots of great choices, including the Campton Place. This is a European-style hotel in two historic buildings, but it is now firmly in the 21st century with chic design, top-quality service and amenities, and an award-winning restaurant. Definitely among the best that the City by the Bay has to offer.

SAN LUIS OBISPO, CA
Moderate
La Cuesta Inn
www.lacuestainn.com
2074 Monterey Street
800/543-2777

Right by a U.S. Route 101 exit and easy to find next to the Days Inn, La Cuesta has its own heated outdoor pool and spa, free wireless internet, a complimentary breakfast, 72 non-smoking rooms with iPod docks, and cable TV with HBO. It's about a 25-minute walk to downtown, or a 5-minute drive. A good mid-price choice, though there are also some Budget and some Expensive rooms too.

Garden Street Inn
www.gardenstreetinn.com
1212 Garden Street
805/545-9802
800/488-2045

Book ahead for the Garden Street Inn. Not only is it a lovely bed-and-breakfast, it's only got nine guest rooms and four suites, and it's also the only place to stay that is right downtown. The inn was built in 1887 and the antique decor reflects that. While it can be a bit noisy because of its central location, the warm welcome and extras like a terrific breakfast and complimentary wine and cheese in the early evening more than make up for that.

Madonna Inn
www.madonnainn.com
100 Madonna Road
805/543-3000
800/543-9666
Even if you don't stay here, you should stop off and pay a visit as there's no hotel anywhere quite like the Madonna Inn. It opened in 1958 and has 110 uniquely decorated rooms, with themes such as the Caveman Room, the Buffalo Room, Antique Cars, Krazy Dazy, Showboat, and even Sir Walter Raleigh. You can buy postcards showing the rooms at the reception, and the hotel also has its own bakery, café, bar/lounge, Alex Madonna's Gold Rush Steak House, a spa, pool, and fitness center. Some Expensive rooms too.

Peach Tree Inn
www.peachtreeinn.com
2001 Monterey Street
805/543-3170
800/227-6396
You can find Budget bargains in low season, and sometimes through special deals, at this country-style inn situated on 1.5 acres near Cuesta County Park, on the edge of San Luis Obispo but still close to downtown. Try for one of the creekside rooms, if you can. All rooms have free wi-fi, and there's a free breakfast, too, as well as a porch with rocking chairs where you can relax and enjoy mountain views. Non-smoking.

SAN SIMEON, CA
Budget
San Simeon Lodge
www.sansimeonrestaurant.com
9520 Castillo Drive
805/927-4601
866/990-8990
This simple lodge is also a beach bar and grill, and while the rooms are basic they're attractively done - and very cheap. It does have a lot of character – and a good setting off the Pacific Coast Highway and right by the sea, near Hearst Castle.

Silver Surf Motel
www.silversurfmotel.com
9390 Castillo Drive
800/621-3999
There aren't too many decent places in San Simeon itself, with a better choice down the road in Cambria. But if you want to be at Hearst Castle when it opens, this is one of the closest budget options. It's right by the beach, and it has 72 rooms, many with ocean views. All have free wireless internet, cable TV, coffee-making facilities, and phones. There are also seven restaurants and cocktail lounges within walking distance, so it's not a bad choice for a budget overnight stop to see Hearst Castle. Some rooms are in the Moderate price range in late spring and summer.

Moderate
Best Western Cavalier Oceanfront Resort
www.cavalierresort.com
415 Hearst Drive
805/927-4688
800/826-8168
This appealing family-owned resort-style motel is, as its name suggests, right by the ocean, in a very attractive location. It's also right on the Pacific Coast Highway, and only three miles from Hearst Castle. There are 90 guest rooms on two floors, it's pet-friendly and children under-12 stay free in their parents' room. It has a range of room types and prices, from Budget to Expensive, varying with the season. Amenities include a heated outdoor pool, a day spa, a restaurant, and 900 feet of its own seafront for guests to enjoy.

San Simeon Pines
www.sspines.com
7200 Moonstone Beach Drive
866/927-4648
Across from San Simeon Beach, and with private beach access, San Simeon Pines is a small resort-style hotel with its own 9-hole par-3 family golf course, croquet, shuffleboard, heated pool, free wireless internet, and complimentary breakfast. The rooms are pleasant and bright, quite spacious, and have wood-burning fireplaces. A good choice in this price range. Non-smoking. No pets.

SANTA BARBARA, CA
Budget
Motel 6 Santa Barbara Beach
www.motel6.com
443 Corona Del Mar Drive
805/564-1392
800/466-8356
The Motel 6 chain started life in Santa Barbara, and there are now several of these motels in and around the town including this one, the original, which still offers basic rooms at Budget prices. Because of the rates and its historic interest it does fill up quickly, so book ahead.

Moderate
Agave Inn
http://agaveinnsb.com
3222 State Street
805/687-6009
The Agave is at the eastern end of the main State Street, about a 5-minute drive to downtown and a 10-minute drive to Stearns Wharf, though it's in a neighborhood with plenty of shops and places to eat. The inn works hard to keep the customers satisfied, with free parking, free wireless internet, a complimentary breakfast, and free use of bicycles. The 13 rooms are decorated with style, using a colorful Spanish theme, and all have flat screen televisions, iPod docks, refrigerators, and microwaves. Some have kitchens too, so ask about availability if you want one.

Franciscan Inn
www.franciscaninn.com
109 Bath Street
805/963-8845
The Franciscan Inn was built in the 1920s in typical Santa Barbara Spanish style with red-tiled rooves, and is one of the friendliest places we've stayed in while driving the Pacific Coast Highway. It's a block back from the beach but also has its own pool, and is only a short walk into the center of Santa Barbara. There are 53 individually decorated rooms arranged around a large courtyard and which are more like hotel rooms than motel rooms. The rates include free parking, free wi-fi, free cookies, and a generous breakfast with freshly-baked rolls and muffins. It didn't surprise us when chatting to

other guests to discover that so many of them were regular visitors and wouldn't stay anywhere else in Santa Barbara. Note that some rooms fall into the Expensive category, mainly on summer weekends, and room rates are cheaper during the week. Read more about this Personal Favorite and see more photos on our website: www.pacific-coast-highway-travel.com/Franciscan_Inn_Santa_Barbara.html.

Franciscan Inn

Harbor House Inn
www.harborhouseinn.com
104 Bath Street
888/474-6789
805/962-9745

Great location, close to PCH, a stone's throw from the waterfront and a five-minute walk to Stearns Wharf. There are 17 rooms and studios, all decorated with antiques and collectibles, which makes the inn feel like a cross between a hotel and a private bed-and-breakfast. There's a welcome basket when you arrive, wireless internet, and free use of the inn's bicycles. You can also borrow beach chairs, beach towels and umbrellas - very helpful if you're doing the PCH road trip and don't want to carry beach gear with you all the way.

The Oceana
www.hoteloceanasantabarbara.com/
202 W. Cabrillo Boulevard
805/965-4577
800/965 9776

The Oceana was easy to find as we drove off PCH to the waterfront, and there it was, midway between Stearn's Wharf and Santa Barbara Harbor, where we'd booked a whale-watching cruise. Walk out of the reception, cross the road and you're on the beach. Perfect! It's a mix of Spanish Mission style and old-fashioned motel, and though some rooms are small they're very colorfully and cheerfully designed. There are also several outdoor relaxing areas with comfortable chairs and tables, two outdoor heated pools, a Jacuzzi and 24-hour fitness center. You can also borrow bikes - cycling around Santa Barbara is very popular. Free wifi, though there is a charge for onsite parking. A Personal Favorite. Read a fuller review on our website: www.pacific-coast-highway-travel.com/Santa-Barbara-Beachfront-Hotel.html.

The Oceana

Expensive

Hyatt Santa Barbara
www.santabarbara.hyatt.com
1111 E. Cabrillo Boulevard
805/963-0744
800/643-1994

Santa Barbara is known for its Spanish Mission-style architecture, and the main hotel building here, built in 1931, reflects that. Room interiors are thoroughly modern, though, and there's a wide range of prices available, including some rooms with ocean views and balconies. Close to the beach on the east end of town, the hotel has a good restaurant and its own bar, spa, gym, and swimming pool.

San Ysidro Ranch
www.sanysidroranch.com
900 San Ysidro Lane, Montecito
805/565-1700
800/368-6788

Ultimate luxury, much favored by celebrities (JFK and Jackie honeymooned here), the ranch is remote and peaceful. It has several very private cottages as well as rooms and suites, and both its restaurant and its bistro serve top quality gourmet fare. Facilities include a swimming pool, gym and a program providing special activities for children.

Simpson House Inn
www.simpsonhouseinn.com
121 E. Arrellaga Street
805/963-7067
800/676-1280

The Simpson House is regularly listed as one of the best bed-and-breakfasts in the USA. The beautiful landscaped gardens cover several acres, yet it's walking distance from downtown. Those gardens conceal several cottages, and there are also rooms in the main Victorian house and barn. In-room spa and massage services are available, and guests also have use of a downtown gym, and bicycles. Its Five Diamond AAA rating make it the only Five Diamond bed and breakfast in the USA.

SANTA CRUZ, CA
Moderate
Babbling Brook Inn
www.babblingbrookinn.com
1025 Laurel Street
831/427-2437
800/866-1131

In complete contrast to the brash boardwalk of central Santa Cruz, the Babbling Brook Inn is everything that its name conjures up – a tranquil retreat, which does have a brook that babbles its way through the redwood and pine trees that surround this historic inn. There are 13 rooms, most with fireplaces and their own private spa tubs, and the inn serves complimentary breakfasts and evening snacks and drinks.

Seaway Inn
www.seawayinn.com
176 West Cliff Drive
831/471-9004
800/493-6220

Perched on a cliff overlooking the bay, and yet close enough to walk to the boardwalk and surfing beaches, the Seaway is a good, compact (18 rooms), mid-range choice. Breakfast, parking, and internet are all complimentary. Some rooms have ocean views (but share balconies) and others have kitchen facilities, so specify what you want before you book. There are some Budget rates available during the week in the off-season.

Expensive
Santa Cruz Dream Inn
www.dreaminnsantacruz.com
175 West Cliff Drive
831/426-4330
866/774-7735

The Dream Inn is right on the beach, so if you want to be close to the surf, and to the boardwalk, this is the place. The 4-star deluxe hotel has 165 rooms, its own oceanfront restaurant, free yoga lessons, a heated pool and children's pool, Jacuzzi, and business center.

SANTA MONICA, CA
Moderate
Sea Shore Motel
www.seashoremotel.com
2637 Main Street
310/392-2787

Two blocks from the beach on Main Street, this is Budget by Santa Monica standards. There are 19 standard rooms, one junior suite and four deluxe suites, ranging in price from just over $100. They are all non-smoking and all have refrigerators, cable TV, free wi-fi, and there's free car parking in their own private lot - in Santa Monica this is a real bonus, especially at this price level.

Expensive
The Embassy Hotel Apartments
www.embassyhotelapts.com
1001 3rd Street
310/394-1279

Not to be confused with the well-known Embassy chain, this wonderful apartment-style hotel is a 1927 Mediterranean-style villa, surrounded by lush gardens with hummingbirds and splashing fountains, and colorful flowers galore. Suites are in the Expensive category but the regular Deluxe Rooms are under $200, a real bargain given the character of the place. In 2001 it was designated a Santa Monica Historic Landmark, and its grand wooden-beamed reception area is very impressive when you enter. Its location, a few blocks from the beach and close to the Third Street Promenade, is also ideal. We loved the gardens, the huge lobby, the antique decor, and the friendliness of the staff, who could not have been more helpful. There's no on-site parking but you receive a parking permit for the street when you check in. Their weekly rates also make it a good place to consider if you're looking for a longer stay than just a few days. You can read more about this Personal Favorite and see more photos on our website: www.pacific-coast-highway-travel.com/Embassy_Hotel_Apartments_Santa_Monica.html.

The Embassy Hotel Apartments

Hotel Shangri-La
www.shangrila-hotel.com
1301 Ocean Avenue
310/394-2791
877/999-1301

The Shangri-La was built in Art Deco style in 1939, closed for a time and then re-opened recently after a huge make-over. The history has been retained but cool contemporary chic has been added, and when it calls itself 'Hollywood on the beach' that seems a fair description. All of the 70 luxury rooms and suites rooms have panoramic ocean views, and it's only a short stroll to Santa Monica Pier. There's a pool (of course!), a fitness center, rooftop bar and lounge, a yoga deck, sidewalk café, and their gourmet restaurant, The Dining Room.

Sheraton Delfina Santa Monica
www.sheratondelfina.com
530 Pico Boulevard
310/399-9344
888/627-8532

The Sheraton Delfina in Santa Monica was a real fun find for us. It had a stylish, boutiquey feel to it without being snobbish or overly expensive. Our 6th floor room had a view down Pico Boulevard to the ocean, and a Jacuzzi on the balcony to enjoy it from. The staff was friendly and efficient, and when we had an emergency to deal with they definitely went the extra mile to help us out - that was the sign of a good hotel, we thought. The Delfina has an outdoor pool just off the classy bar area, with its colorful collection of bottles. You can also have a casual meal here (our steaks were mouthwateringly wonderful), and there's another café/restaurant and a lobby bar too. A new Personal Favorite for us, and you can see and read more about our visit here: www.pacific-coast-highway-travel.com/Santa_Monica_Luxury_Hotels.html.

Sheraton Delfina Santa Monica

Shutters on the Beach
www.shuttersonthebeach.com
1 Pico Boulevard
310/458-0030
800/334-9000
Shutters *is* right on the beach, just to the south of Santa Monica Pier. Although there are almost 200 luxury rooms and suites, it manages to feel more intimate, with a very relaxing, casual chic atmosphere. Amenities include two restaurants, bar, gym, spa, guest bicycles, and a pool for those who don't want to walk a few yards to the beach.

SEASIDE, OR
Budget
Oceanfront Motel
www.oceanfrontor.com
50 1st Avenue
503/738-5661
866/808-5661
If you want simple, clean, cheap, and right on the beach, this is the place. There are 35 rooms and suites accommodating from one to six people, and all rooms have fridge, microwave, and coffee-makers. No pets.

Moderate
Gilbert Inn
www.gilbertinn.com
341 Beach Drive
503/738-9770
800/410-9770
Built in 1892, the Gilbert Inn is for anyone who likes a historic and romantic place to stay. All the rooms have free wireless internet, queen-sized beds, and flat-screen TVs with cable. It's only one block to Main Street, a short walk to the beach, and two minutes off U.S. Route 101 as it goes through Seaside. Rates go from Budget to Expensive.

Seaside Oceanfront Inn
www.theseasideinn.com
581 South Prom
503/738.6403
800/772-7766
Rooms range from Budget to Expensive, depending on the room and the season. There are some bargains to be had if you don't mind a partial view, or will settle for a mountain view rather than a sea view. This welcoming bed-and-breakfast has 14 themed rooms and suites, and it's right on the oceanfront. The best rooms have large windows that take full advantage of the views, and the inn also has its own restaurant, Oceanfront Dining on the Prom (known to locals as Maggie's on the Prom). Some rooms fall into the Expensive category in summer and at weekends.

Expensive
Rivertide Suites
www.rivertidesuites.com
102 N. Holladay
503/436-2241
888/777-4047
Great location on the Necanicum River for this condominium hotel with 45 rooms/suites and its own pool, though the beach is only a short walk away. There's also a hot tub, exercise room, and complimentary breakfast, newspaper, and manager's reception every night. It's possible to get some of the smaller rooms, and the studios, for Moderate prices.

SEATTLE, WA
Budget
Moore Hotel
www.moorehotel.com
1926 2nd Avenue
206/448-4851
800/421-5508
At the budget end of the scale yet close to Pike Place Market, the rooms at the Moore are mainly basic (with a few exceptions) and definitely aimed at the younger traveler. If you accept that, then you can stay close to downtown Seattle for a real bargain rate, even for the rooms with private bathrooms. Even cheaper are those which share a bathroom, but there are also suites in the Moderate price range.

Moderate
Executive Hotel Pacific
www.pacificplazahotel.com
400 Spring Street
206/623-3900
888/388-3932
The Executive is one of the cheaper downtown options that's still a pleasant place to stay, located about five blocks back from the waterfront. It has 154 rooms and suites, and prices for some of the better rooms can be in the Expensive category so check the room rates when booking. Amenities include a restaurant, coffee bar, business center, and exercise room.

Gaslight Inn
www.gaslight-inn.com
1727 15th Avenue
206/325-3654
Built in 1906, the Gaslight Inn is in the Capitol Hill district and delightfully decorated with Arts and Crafts furniture, making for a really pleasant (and child-free) place to stay. There's a heated outdoor pool in summer, and there are also some budget rooms with shared bathrooms. Minimum two-night stay in the summer.

Pensione Nichols
www.pensionenichols.com
1923 1st Avenue
206/441-7125
There are some affordable downtown options if you're in Seattle on a budget, such as this small, historic bed-and-breakfast. You have to sacrifice some comforts, and most rooms share bathrooms, though there are also two suites with private bathrooms, but the place is very well-run.

Expensive
Alexis Hotel
www.alexishotel.com
1007 1st Avenue
206/624-4844
888/850-1155
The Alexis is a terrifically stylish hotel in a great downtown location, based in two historic buildings just back from the waterfront. It has its own restaurant and bar, along with a gym and a spa, and all the rooms have original works of art, adding to the sophisticated feel of the place. It was listed by *Travel+Leisure* magazine as one of the Top 500 Hotels in the World.

Edgewater
www.edgewaterhotel.com
Pier 67, 2411 Alaskan Way
206/728-7000
800/624-0670
The only Seattle luxury hotel that is right on the water, built over one of the piers, the Edgewater has a rustic-style decor to contrast its urban setting. Views range from the distant Olympic Mountains to

the Space Needle, and its award-winning Six Seven restaurant is one of the best seafood places in Seattle. Four Diamond AAA rating.

Hotel 1000
www.hotel1000seattle.com
1000 1st Avenue
206/932-3102
Several publications have rated the Hotel 1000 as one of the best hotels in the world, and it's easy to see why when you arrive. The lobby has cool, clean, stylish lines, with subtle lighting and striking artwork on the walls. By contrast the BOKA Restaurant has plenty of plush bright reds and swirling shapes, creating a livelier feel. The rooms too have very clean lines, intriguing artwork and comforting colors. Some have stunning views from large picture windows, and they also have every gadget known to man, including some you'd never have thought of. There is also an excellent bar, gym, and spa facilities. Yet despite all this, and unlike many modern hip hotels, the style never gets in the way of the functionality. It's fun and cool but everything also works!

Hotel Monaco
www.monaco-seattle.com
1101 4th Avenue
206/621-1770
800/945-2240
The Monaco chain of hotels carved out an early name for themselves as reliably hip, boutique places to stay. The one in Seattle is no exception, with Monaco trademarks such as a daily wine reception, complimentary morning coffee and tea, a free shoeshine, and the option to have a pet goldfish in your room, just for the fun of it. There's also a visit by a fortune teller twice a week! The rooms are modern and stylishly decorated, each one different but all with a fun feel to them. They have city views, some have 2-person jetted tubs, with an in-room spa service including a yoga mat to use during your stay. The Monaco chain is decidedly different and we love them.

SEAVIEW, WA
Moderate
The Shelburne Inn
www.shelburneinn.com
Pacific Way and 45th Street
360/642-2442
800/466-1896
The Shelburne has 14 rooms and suites and is definitely one of the best choices for the Long Beach area. Built in 1896, it's said to be Washington's oldest continuously run hotel, and provides attractive rooms (some with balconies) at reasonable rates. It also has its own Shelburne Spa, a good restaurant plus an English-style pub.

SEQUIM, WA
Budget
Sequim West Inn and RV Park
www.sequimwestinn.com
740 W. Washington Street
360/683-4144
800/528-4527
You have a range of options here, including motel rooms, larger suites, and cottages to rent as well as the 27-space RV Park. All the rooms have cable TV, phone, microwaves, refrigerators, hair dryers, and coffee. Cottages are for larger groups with two or three bedrooms and one or two bathrooms. Simple but comfortable accommodation at very good rates.

Moderate
Diamond Point Inn Bed and Breakfast
www.diamondpointinn.com
241 Sunshine Road
360/797-7720
800/310-6322
This is a lovely place with ten acres of its own grounds, and days begin with a memorable five-course breakfast which includes treats like fresh-baked cinnamon rolls and muffins, and two main entrées. Amenities include free use of mountain bikes to explore this part of the Olympic Peninsula, a Jacuzzi, free wi-fi, and a baby grand piano for musical guests to enjoy playing. Accommodation is in a range of rooms and private cottages, pleasingly decorated in old-fashioned

style but with different themes: butterflies, artistic, golfing, and angling among them.

Juan de Fuca Cottages
www.juandefuca.com
182 Marine Drive
360/683-4433
866/683-4433
Prices can range from the Budget to the Expensive, but are mostly Moderate in this collection of cottages and suites on a bluff, and sharing a coastline with the National Wildlife Refuge. The rooms are nicely done and all feature watercolor works by a local artist. They also have whirlpool tubs, views of either water or mountains, and include the use of a private beach. Kayaks and bicycles can be rented too.

STINSON BEACH, CA
Moderate
Stinson Beach Motel
www.stinsonbeachmotel.com
3416 State Route #1
415/868-1712
This old-fashioned motel has only eight units, all of which have been modernized inside, making for an excellent and affordable place to stay. You might even get a Budget-rate room at some periods of the year. The rooms surround three garden courtyards, and the gardens are lush and colorful. While amenities may be basic, this is a characterful accommodation option in this beautiful part of the Pacific Coast just north of San Francisco.

TILLAMOOK, OR
Moderate
Sandlake Country Inn
www.sandlakecountryinn.com
8505 Galloway Road
503/965-6745
877/726-3525
This farmhouse bed-and-breakfast has three suites and one private cottage, with features including fireplaces, canopy beds, and antique furnishings. All rooms have TVs, DVDs and bathrooms with

whirlpool tubs and showers. The inn is on the Oregon Historic Registry and is a delightful rural retreat.

VENTURA, CA
Budget
Vagabond Inn Ventura
www.vagabondinn-ventura-hotel.com
756 E. Thompson Blvd.
800/522-1555
805/648-5371
Two minutes off U.S. Route 101, this modestly priced place is very central (two blocks from the Historic Old Town) and one of the best options if you're on a budget. It offers free breakfast, daily newspaper on weekdays, a heated pool, free parking, pet-friendly rooms, its own spa, and discounts for seniors. Some rooms are in the Moderate price range.

Moderate
Pierpont Inn
www.pierpontinn.com
550 Sanjon Road
805/643-6144
800/285-4667
Set on a headland away from downtown, the historic Pierpont Inn (first built in 1910 and later renovated) has 77 rooms, suites, and cottages. It also has a first-rate restaurant with a wonderful view of the coast and of Ventura. Guests can use the nearby Pierpont Racquet Club where there are pools, tennis and racquetball courts, and fitness and spa facilities.

WALDPORT, OR
Moderate
Cliff House Bed-and-Breakfast
www.cliffhouseoregon.com
1450 Adahi Road
541/563-2506
There are views of Oregon's white-sand beaches from the four rooms in this intimate and historic bed-and-breakfast, with its antique furnishings and wood-burning stoves. There's a fabulous deck from where you can watch seals and sea lions, as well as seeing the sun go down. They also have a hot tub, and massages can be booked too.

WESTPORT, WA
Budget
Tokeland Hotel
www.tokelandhotel.com
100 Hotel Road, Tokeland
360/267-7006
About 15 miles south of Westport and overlooking Willapa Bay, the Tokeland is the oldest resort hotel in the state. It's also one of the best bargains around, especially in winter when rooms were under $50 at the time of writing. For that price don't expect private bathrooms, as the house goes back to 1885. Rooms are decorated in Victorian style and the whole place is really relaxing. It has its own dining room where guests can enjoy breakfast (complimentary), lunch, and dinner every day except Monday and Tuesday.

Moderate
Chateau Westport
www.chateauwestport.com
710 West Hancock Avenue
360/268-9101
800/255-9101
Normally rooms here are in the Moderate range, but theree are also larger suites that are in the Expensive category. The place itself is an unusual combination – a motel that does look a little like a chateau. Many of the rooms have balconies with ocean views, and facilities include fridges, microwaves, free wi-fi, and complimentary breakfast. It's right by the beach, but if the weather cuts up rough there's a hot tub and a heated indoor pool.

Harbor Resort
www.harborresort.com
861 Neddie Rose Drive
360/268-0169
The Harbor Resort offers seven rooms, seven cottages, and some condos too. It's in a delightful setting overlooking the ocean, making for great wildlife-watching opportunities. Room prices range from Budget to Expensive, depending on type of room and time of year, but most have Moderate rates.

YACHATS, OR
Budget
Fireside Motel
www.firesidemotel.com
1881 US 101 N.
800/336-3573
On U.S. Route 101 less than a mile north of the center of Yachats, the Fireside has 43 units. You can get oceanside and oceanview rooms, as the motel stands between U.S. Route 101 and the sea, leading onto the oceanfront walking trail. Some rooms are Budget, others Moderate. Non-smoking. Pet-friendly.

See Vue
www.seevue.com
95590 Route 101
541/547-3227
866/547-3237
In season most rooms edge up into the Moderate category, but otherwise this is one of the cheaper places to stay in the area. Though it's a few miles south of Yachats center, the plus side is its location on a cliff overlooking the ocean. The See Vue has 11 rooms and they all have great views. Some have fireplaces, too. Each has a different design theme including Santa Fe, the Far East, Crow's Nest, and The Vineyard. Pet-friendly. Non-smoking.

Moderate/Expensive
Overleaf Lodge and Spa
www.overleaflodge.com
280 Overleaf Lodge Lane
541/547-4880
The layout of this splendid lodge ensures that all 54 rooms enjoy ocean views, and you can walk right out onto the beaches and explore the tide pools. We loved this location, and the fact that we could relax in our room and watch families exploring the tide pools, or just walking and admiring this gorgeous stretch of coast line. There's a lovely, welcoming lobby, where the buffet breakfast is served. The rooms are spacious and ours even had a bath with a view! There's no restaurant, but it's only a short drive into Yachats, which has plenty of options. Rooms divide between Moderate and Expensive prices. A Personal Favorite. See the full review on our website: www.pacific-coast-highway-travel.com/Overleaf_Lodge_Yachats.html.

Overleaf Lodge and Spa

CALIFORNIA WINE COUNTRY

PASO ROBLES
Moderate

Adelaide Inn
www.adelaideinn.com
1215 Ysabel Avenue, Paso Robles
800/549-7276
South of the town center and just a few minutes off US Route 101, the Adelaide Inn has 65 wineries and wine-tasting opportunities within a 30-minute drive. It's been in business for over 45 years, which is a measure of its reliability. It has 108 rooms that offer very good value for money, and there's a solar-heated outdoor pool, miniature golf, sauna, fitness room, free high-speed internet, free newspapers, free parking, and many other features that make this one of the best inexpensive options in the area.

La Bellasera
www.labellasera.com
206 Alexa Court
805/238-2834
The Bellasera is right by U.S. Route 101, where it merges with State Route 46, the road that leads down to the coast and PCH. It has 60 large rooms and suites, and prices range from Moderate to Expensive, depending on the room and time of year, so be sure to check room rates first. It's south of the town center, which is a 10-minute drive away, but if you don't want to drive it has its own Enoteca restaurant and bar, and there are some other eating options nearby. All rooms have deluxe bathrooms with walk-in showers, HDTVs, free high-speed internet, and iPod/MP3 docking stations.

Paso Robles Inn
www.pasoroblesinn.com
1103 Spring Street
805/238-2660
800/676-1713
If you want to be in the heart of Paso Robles, there are few better places. The inn overlooks the City Park and has been welcoming travelers for over a century now. It therefore has a lovely period feel, but it also offers a heated outdoor pool in the beautiful gardens, in-room spa treatments, and its own restaurant, the excellent Paso

Robles Inn Steakhouse. Some of the better rooms have hot springs mineral tubs either in the room or on the private patio, and a recent renovation has improved the property enormously.

Expensive
Hotel Cheval
www.hotelcheval.com
1021 Pine Street
805/226-9995
866/522-6999
Right in the town center, close to City Park, the Cheval has only 16 rooms and this boutique luxury hotel is definitely one of the best places to stay in Paso Robles itself. The stylish and contemporary rooms come with complimentary breakfast, wireless internet, newspaper, bottled water, and organic chocolates with the turn-down service. The hotel has its own SUV which guests can book to do wine tours in comfort. Although it doesn't have its own restaurant, there is a bar, as well as fine dining on the doorstep in Paso Robles itself.

JUST Inn Bed and Breakfast
www.justinwine.com
11680 Chimney Rock Road
805/238-6932
800/726-0049
About 20 miles west of town, this is your chance to stay on a vineyard. The JUSTIN Vineyards and Winery is also the home of the JUST Inn Bed and Breakfast, and very stylish it is, too. There are only four sumptuous suites, with tapestry-covered furnishings and frescoed ceilings, while the usual hotel extras are added to here with a complimentary bottle of fine wine from the vineyard, and a free winery tour. We couldn't believe how sumptuous our room, the Sussex Suite (see photo), was, and the vineyard tour and wine tasting were excellent. The Inn also has the gourmet Deborah's Room restaurant, which is one of the best we've eaten in anywhere in the USA. With its own chef catering to only a handful of tables, it is a truly memorable dining experience - and with great wine too, of course! Definitely a Personal Favorite, and a great highlight of our drive. You can read more, and see more photos, here: www.pacific-coast-highway-travel.com/Paso_Robles_Accommodation.html.

The JUST Inn

The Summerwood Inn
www.summerwoodwine.com
2175 Arbor Road
805/227-1111
About five miles south of the town center, and just off State Route 41, the Summerwood Inn is part of the Summerwood Winery and makes for a peaceful and romantic retreat. There are only nine rooms and they all have private balconies that look out over the vineyards. Rates include a gourmet breakfast, an afternoon wine tasting with hors d'oeuvres, and a range of desserts in the evening.

Villa Valdemosa
www.villavaldemosa.com/
2552 Old Grove Lane
805/237-0170
The Villa Valdemosa is a 15-minute drive southeast of the center of Paso Robles. The guest rooms are spacious and elegant. The best, the Bordeaux Suite, has a four-poster bed and a his/hers bathroom with a soaking tub offering views across the surrounding vineyards. There is a complimentary breakfast and afternoon wine tasting, and monthly music concerts, too. The Valdemosa doesn't have its own

restaurant, but there is a good choice within a short drive of the property.

SONOMA VALLEY
Moderate
Beltane Ranch
www.beltaneranch.com
11775 Sonoma Highway, Glen Ellen
707/996-6501
The Beltane is still a working ranch, a five-minute drive north from Glen Ellen town center. Don't think of cowboys on the prairie, though. Think instead of gorgeous gardens, a private tennis court, exhilarating walking trails from the historic 1893 property, free wireless internet, and five intimate guest rooms and one cottage, decorated with antiques and with works from local artists. Some rooms are in the Expensive range.

Best Western Sonoma Valley Inn
http://sonomavalleyinn.com
550 Second Street West, Sonoma
707/938-9200
One block from Sonoma Plaza, the Best Western shows you can get good quality accommodation, and character, from a chain name. Rooms have fireplaces and private balconies or patios. There's a heated outdoor pool, sauna, steam room, Jacuzzi, two spa rooms for treatments and massages, a complimentary breakfast, and free wireless internet. Non-smoking. Pet-friendly. Children under-16 free of charge. Some rooms are in the Expensive category.

El Pueblo Inn
www.elpuebloinn.com
896 West Napa Street, Sonoma
707/996-3651
800/900-8844
The El Pueblo Inn has a range of rooms and prices, and while they're mostly Moderate you can also pick up a Budget rate in its cheaper rooms if you're going out of season. It's simple but central, about a 20-minute walk or a 2-minute drive to City Hall. The inn opened in 1959 as a ranch-style hotel built with adobe, and today it retains a slightly dated feel, but in the nicest way. There's a heated outdoor pool with a hot tub, and other amenities include a fitness room, free

breakfast, free internet in the public areas, and free parking. No smoking inside the buildings.

Fern Grove Cottages
www.ferngrove.com
16650 Highway 116, Guerneville
888/243-2674
In the heart of the Russian River Valley, Fern Grove began life as a small resort in the 1920s. Its rooms are fairly simple but they do offer a good budget choice in the mainly pricey wine country. There are studios, one-bedroom and two-bedroom suites, and three cottages to choose from, at a range of prices in the Moderate category. It's got a lovely location, surrounded by redwoods and a few minutes' walk west of the center of town. It has its own pool and sun deck, free high-speed internet, and a complimentary breakfast. Pets are welcome by prior arrangement.

Sonoma Creek Inn
http://sonomacreekinn.com
239 Boyes Boulevard, Sonoma
707/939-9463
888/712-1289
A 5-minute drive from the center of Sonoma in the Boyes Hot Springs area, the Sonoma Creek Inn has 16 rooms. Though mainly in the Moderate price range, there are some Budget rates available when it's not so busy. Some of the rooms have private patios or porches, and all have fridges, free wi-fi vaulted ceilings, cable TV, and tasteful but fun antique furnishings.

Sonoma Hotel
www.sonomahotel.com
110 W. Spain Street, Sonoma
800/468-6016
Locations don't come any better than right on the historic Sonoma Plaza, where the 19th-century Sonoma Hotel has 16 guest rooms and suites. They all have French country furniture, and come at a range of prices. Book for two nights out of season and some rooms come into the Budget price range (just), while others creep into the Expensive category. All rooms have their own bathrooms, cable TV, and phones, and there is a complimentary breakfast and daily wine tasting.

Expensive
Camellia Inn
www.camelliainn.com
211 North Street, Healdsburg
707/433-8182
800/727-8182
This 1859 property is very central yet has lovely gardens. It gets its name from the 50 types of camellia that are grown here, and you can take a self-guided tour of the gardens. There's a floral theme throughout the house too, but while the feel is gently historic, the amenities are all modern. Surprisingly for an intimate bed-and-breakfast with only nine rooms (some at Moderate prices), the Camellia has its own swimming pool, and guests can also enjoy a complimentary breakfast and daily wine tasting. The owners have a vineyard, which began when wine was first made at the inn itself.

Fairmont Sonoma Mission Inn and Spa
www.fairmont.com/sonoma/
100 Boyes Boulevard, Sonoma
707/938-9000
866/540-4499
In the Boyes Hot Springs area a few minutes' drive from the center of town, the Fairmont feels like it would be just as much at home on the California coast. The recently modernized resort spreads over 12 acres, with 226 rooms and suites. The grandest of these costs over $1200 a night, but there are plenty nearer the $200 mark, too. Rates include breakfast, an afternoon wine tasting, and a complimentary bottle of Sonoma wine when you arrive. It has its own spa, an 18-hole championship golf course, impressive business facilities, and its Santé Restaurant has even won a Michelin star. Definitely Sonoma in style.

Gaige House Inn
www.gaige.com
13540 Arnold Drive, Glen Ellen
707/935-0237
800/935-0237
The Gaige House has been called the best bed-and-breakfast anywhere in Sonoma or Napa, and that is praise indeed. It oozes cool elegance, with a serene and simplistic Asian-inspired decor. Some rooms have their own private Zen gardens. *Condé Nast Traveler* rates it

as one of the best small hotels in the world. It has its own spa and swimming pool, and guests can join evening wine tastings with the wine-makers. The inn is not really suited for children or pets.

H2 Hotel
www.h2hotel.com
219 Healdsburg Avenue, Healdsburg
707/922-5251
This hip new hotel is right in the center of Healdsburg, and is the kind of place you'll find in many of the world's major cities, but not usually in Wine Country. It's got a 'living' roof, is ultra eco-friendly, and features unusual art works throughout the hotel. Guests can enjoy a solar-heated pool, free 3-hour bike rentals, weekly yoga classes, free wireless internet, a complimentary light breakfast, and a DVD library. It's definitely different - not for the more traditional traveler but great fun.

Inn at Sonoma
www.innatsonoma.com
630 Broadway, Sonoma
707/939-1340
888/568-9818
Two blocks from the central Sonoma Plaza, the inn is a newer hotel with 19 guest bedrooms. Room rates include breakfast, an afternoon wine tasting with hors d'oeuvres, free wireless internet, free covered parking, fresh-baked cookies, a newspaper, use of the rooftop hot tub, and use of their bicycles to take the bike path to the nearest wineries.

Ledson Hotel
http://ledsonhotel.com
480 First Street East, Sonoma
707/996-9779
The Ledson is a new luxury hotel built right on the Sonoma Plaza but in Victorian style, so it blends in effortlessly. There are only six guest bedrooms, all of them large and all of them with balconies. They also have king-sized beds, antique furnishings, whirlpool baths, free internet, and many other amenities. Note that entry to the hotel is through the Harmony Lounge, which is part of the hotel and where breakfast is served. There is no formal reception area.

MacArthur Place
www.macarthurplace.com
29 East MacArthur Street, Sonoma
707/938-2929
800/722-1866
A few blocks south of Sonoma Plaza, MacArthur Place is a spa resort that has been made out of a Victorian-era hotel. The original building is from the 1850s and is one of the oldest homes in Sonoma. There are now 64 rooms, suites and cottages throughout seven acres of grounds, which also contain the Garden Spa and Fitness Center, a heated pool, and whirlpool. Here you'll also find the Saddles Steakhouse, which has been voted Best Restaurant in California and also has an outstanding list of local wines.

Renaissance Lodge at Sonoma Resort and Spa
www.thelodgeatsonoma.com
1325 Broadway, Sonoma
707/935-6600
866/263-0758
At the southern end of town where Broadway meets the Napa Road, this luxurious spa resort is another of those that could equally well be found on the California coast. There are 10 acres of gardens, which contain the Cottage Rooms. Other rooms are in the main lodge building, and there are also a handful of more spacious suites available. The lodge has its own Raindance Spa and the Carneros Bistro and Wine Bar, which rates among the top restaurants in the Bay Area. There are also weekly wine tasting and wine education events.

Vintners Inn
www.vintnersinn.com
4350 Barnes Road, Santa Rosa
707/575-7350
800/421-2584
Just off U.S. Route 101 north of Santa Rosa, and convenient for the Charles M. Schulz Sonoma County Airport, the Vintners Inn is surrounded by 92 acres of its own vineyards. It has 44 rooms (including six suites), the highly acclaimed John Ash & Co. restaurant, the Courtyard Spa Room, and all the other top-class amenities you would expect from an intimate luxury hotel.

NAPA VALLEY
Budget
Calistoga Inn
www.calistogainn.com
1250 Lincoln Ave, Calistoga
707/942-4101

If you want to explore Napa Valley but you're really on a budget, then the Calistoga Inn is worth considering. The prices are among the cheapest around, but obviously you don't get luxury. There are 18 rooms which all have a sink, but you have to share a bathroom down the corridor: there are separate restrooms/shower rooms for men and women. Otherwise, the rooms are clean and small, and you have the lively microbrewery bar and restaurant right below you. Note that the Inn was closed after a fire in August 2012 but hopes to re-open on May 1st, 2013.

Motel 6 Napa Valley
www.motel6.com
3380 Solano Avenue, Napa
707/257-6111

This is one of the cheaper Napa options, and as Napa isn't a cheap place you have to accept some compromises if you're looking for Budget accommodation. The inn (formerly the Napa Valley Redwood Inn) offers perfectly good, standard motel-style rooms, with lots of complimentary extras such as newspapers, wireless internet, parking, and breakfast. There's also a pool in the summer. The down side is that it's close to Highway 29 so it gets some noise, and you have to drive into Napa town center (or take a 30-minute walk). Non-smoking.

Wine Valley Lodge
www.winevalleylodge.com
200 South Coombs, Napa
707/224-7911
800/696-7911

The Wine Valley Lodge is another cheap Napa option, if you are happy with simple motel-style accommodation and don't mind the short drive into the town center to get where the action is. There are 54 rooms that look out on the swimming pool, and breakfast and wireless internet are both included in the economic room rates. The Lodge was good enough in the past for Elvis Presley and Marilyn

Monroe to have stayed there, alongside several other famous names. Some rooms are Moderate and even Expensive, so check room rates when booking. Rooms are all non-smoking.

Moderate
Carlin Cottages
www.carlincottages.com
1623 Lake Street, Calistoga
707/942-9102
800/734-4624
These Calistoga country cottages are reasonably close to the center of town and offer a range of rooms and prices. These run from mini-suites, where you might find a bargain midweek in winter, through to large two-bedroom suites, which rate as Expensive at weekends. There's an outdoor pool and outdoor Jacuzzi, both fed by hot springs, and all rooms come with free wireless internet. Non-smoking. No pets.

Napa Winery Inn
www.napawineryinn.com
1998 Trower Avenue, Napa
800/522-8999
The hotel is a 5-minute drive north of the center of Napa on Highway 29, and offers a wide range of room types and prices, from simple studio-style to deluxe doubles. They all come with free wireless internet, breakfast, and cable TV, and guests also have the use of the courtyard swimming pool and whirlpool spa. For easy dining, Marie Callender's Restaurant and Bakery is right next door.

Petit Logis
www.petitlogis.com
6527 Yount Street, Yountville
707/944-2332
877/944-2332
If you want to eat in some of Napa Valley's finest restaurants, then the Petit Logis is the place to be, as several of the best, including the French Laundry, are within easy walking distance. This country-style inn doesn't serve breakfast but there are several breakfast options nearby, including the Bouchon Bakery which is right next door. The standards at the Petit Logis are impressive, though at weekends and in summer room rates go up into the Expensive category. There are

only five rooms, and although they are very different they all include a bathroom with double Jacuzzi, a fireplace, refrigerator, TV, and wireless internet.

Expensive
1801 First
www.1801first.com
1801 First Street, Napa
707/224-3739
800/518-0146
This stylish bed-and-breakfast, walking distance from the center of Napa town, was designed in 1903 by one of Napa's leading architects, William Corlett. The owners have retained that period feel and style, while incorporating modern amenities like high-speed internet, Jacuzzis, and video and CD libraries. There's a daily wine tasting with hors d'oeuvres, and the breakfast is one of the best we've had anywhere. All rooms are luxury suites, and in addition there are two cottages and the Carriage House in the lovely, private rear gardens. This is definitely one of our Personal Favorites and you can see more on our website: www.pacific-coast-highway-travel.com/Napa-Bed-and-Breakfast.html.

1801 First

Auberge du Soleil
www.aubergedusoleil.com
180 Rutherford Hill Road, Rutherford
707/963-1211
800/348-5406
The Auberge is one of the best-known - and best - luxury resorts in the whole Napa Valley. It's the kind of place where celebrities hang out, and rooms here cost serious money. The Auberge spreads over the terraces of a hillside, with wonderful views over Napa Valley, and its amenities include a 7000-square-foot spa, the highly acclaimed Auberge du Soleil Restaurant, the separate Bistro & Bar, a fitness center, tennis, swimming pool, steam room, an outdoor sculpture gallery and much more. Accommodations range from the smallest rooms (420 sq. ft.) in the main house to private mansions.

La Belle Epoque
www.napaboutiqueinn.com
1386 Calistoga Avenue, Napa
707/257-2161
800/238-8070
The centrally located Belle Epoque is a boutique inn in a Victorian home. Room rates include a gourmet breakfast, evening wine tasting, a wine passport, and wireless internet. Massages are available in the secluded garden or in your room, and the rooms themselves are tastefully decorated in an old-fashioned style, some having four-poster beds, and ranging in price from Moderate to Expensive.

Cedar Gables Inn
www.cedargablesinn.com
486 Coombs Street, Napa
707/224-7969
800/309/7969
Cedar Gables describes itself as a bed-and-breakfast mansion, and it is a large place, big enough for them also to hold cookery schools here. It was built in 1892 in Tudor style and is very central, just down from 5th Street and close to the river. The inn's bar is called the Old English Tavern and here there's a complementary wine (or beer) tasting each evening, with appetizers and occasional live music, too. There are nine rooms decorated in Victorian style, and it's quite a place to stay if you like historic atmospheres.

Maison Fleurie
www.maisonfleurienapa.com
6529 Yount Street, Yountville
707/944-2056
800/788-0369
The Maison Fleurie brings a touch of French country style to the center of Yountville. On the doorstep is the Bouchon restaurant, and other top Napa dining is within a short stroll. There are 13 guest bedrooms all decorated in different styles and based in three cottages around a courtyard. If you don't mind a small room they are in the Moderate price range, but the larger rooms are worth paying a little extra for. All rooms come with complimentary breakfast, cookies, wireless internet, a newspaper, free parking, and an afternoon wine-tasting with appetizers. Other amenities include an outdoor pool and hot tub.

Meadowood
www.meadowood.com
900 Meadowood Lane, St. Helena
800/458-8080
A 5-minute drive north of the center of St. Helena is Meadowood, a luxury resort of some 250 acres that was rated the best in Napa Valley by readers of *Travel+Leisure* magazine. The rooms are divided among 20 different lodges that spread around the lovely rural setting. They range from regular 2-room apartments through to large estate suites and family lodges. Amenities include two restaurants, the Health Spa, seven tennis courts, a 4.5-mile hiking trail, croquet, a 9-hole golf course, an adult swimming pool and a family pool, too.

Milliken Creek Inn and Spa
www.millikencreekinn.com
1815 Silverado Trail, Napa
707/255-1197
800/835-6112
The Silverado Trail is a scenic trail that runs for 29 miles through the Napa Valley, passing through Napa itself on the east side of the river. The Milliken Creek Inn is a 5-star luxury hotel set in three acres in an excellent location on the very edge of Napa town and close to the river. In fact the Milliken Creek Spa is right by the river. The inn has only 12 rooms, giving it that extra feel of intimacy, and they are all designed differently but with a common approach of chic and

simple. The least expensive rooms are the Milliken Rooms, but if you pay a little more then the Deluxe Rooms offer river views, while the Luxury rooms have riverside locations, and most have terraces or decks.

Napa River Inn
www.napariverinn.com
500 Main Street, Napa
877/251-8500
A member of the Historic Hotels of America, the inn is based at the Napa Mill, an 1884 Victorian riverside complex, which means you'll have restaurants, shops and entertainment right on your doorstep - though the center of Napa is only a short walk away. There is a wide range of room choices, from standard to luxury suites, based in three different buildings. The best are in the original 1884 Hatt building, with others in the 1862 Embarcadero Building, and the rest in the 32-room Plaza Hotel Building. Rates include breakfast delivered to your room, daily wine-tasting, weekday newspaper, and wireless internet.

Red Door Inn
www.reddoornapa.com
1523 Main Street, St. Helena
707/963-5400
This bed-and-breakfast is in the very center of St. Helena and has just three superb rooms. The Bambou is a separate one-bedroom studio overlooking the courtyard and with its own balcony; the Ciel is on its own on the second level of the main house and has a fireplace and a dedicated parking space outside, while the Coeur is in the heart of the main house and requires on-street parking. All have free wi-fi, breakfast, and wine and cheese each afternoon. St. Helena's downtown restaurants are all within a few minutes' walk.

Wine Country Inn
www.winecountryinn.com
1152 Lodi Lane, St. Helena
707/963-7077
888/465-4608
Two miles outside St. Helena along Highway 29 is this wonderful retreat which has 20 regular rooms, four suites, and five luxury cottages. The complimentary afternoon appetizers that come with the wine-tasting, and the gourmet breakfast dishes, are all so good

that the inn has the recipes ready to hand to guests who are always asking for them. All the cottages have private patios which overlook the neighboring vineyards. They also have fireplaces, king-sized beds, 800 sq ft of space, and a two-person Jacuzzi tub. We loved the extra little touches in our room, like a reading nook and a beautiful stained glass window over the bath, which gave the room a lovely romantic colored lighting. There is no restaurant at the inn so you will need to drive or to book the courtesy restaurant shuttle that goes to several of the area's best eating places. However, the inn does do special dinners from time to time throughout the year, so ask when booking. This is very definitely one of our Personal Favorite places. We didn't want to leave, and you can see and read why on our website: www.pacific-coast-highway-travel.com/Napa-Wine-Country-Inn.html.

Mike Having Coffee at the Wine Country Inn

North-South List of Places with Recommended Hotels

Washington North

A   Seattle
B   Port Townsend
C   Sequim
D   Port Angeles
E   Forks
F   Olympic National Park (Lake Quinault)

Washington South

A   Aberdeen
B   Westport
C   Long Beach
D   Seaview
E   Ilwaco

Oregon North

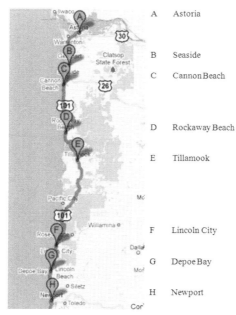

A   Astoria

B   Seaside

C   Cannon Beach

D   Rockaway Beach

E   Tillamook

F   Lincoln City

G   Depoe Bay

H   Newport

Oregon South

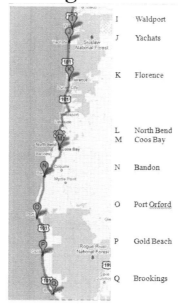

I   Waldport

J   Yachats

K   Florence

L   North Bend
M   Coos Bay

N   Bandon

O   Port Orford

P   Gold Beach

Q   Brookings

Northern California:
Crescent City to Stinson Beach

A Crescent City

B Arcata
C Eureka
D Ferndale

E Fort Bragg
F Mendocino

G Gualala

H Bodega Bay
I Point Reyes

J Stinson Beach

California:
San Francisco to Big Sur

A San Francisco

B Half Moon Bay

C Santa Cruz

D Pacific Grove
E Monterey
F Carmel-by-the-Sea

G Big Sur

California: San Simeon to Santa Monica

A   San Simeon (for Hearst Castle)
B   Cambria (for Hearst Castle)
C   Cayucos
D   Morro Bay
E   San Luis Obispo
F   Pismo Beach
G   Santa Barbara
H   Ventura
I   Santa Monica

California: Los Angeles to San Diego

A   Los Angeles

B   Huntington Beach
C   Newport Beach
D   Laguna Beach
E   Dana Point

F   Carlsbad
G   Del Mar
H   La Jolla
I   San Diego
J   Coronado

As well as longer hotel reviews, you can find full information about the Pacific Coast Highway drive on our website: www.Pacific-Coast-Highway-Travel.com

Here you'll find details about driving times and distances, the best time of year to go, what to do in the various stops on the way, which guidebooks to buy, where to go whale-watching, and even information on cheap flights to the main cities along the Pacific Coast Highway. There's also a contact page where we're happy to answer your questions, to help make your PCH road trip perfect!

If you've found this book useful, please consider posting a review on Amazon, so that others can know what to expect. And if you have any suggestions for improving it, then email us and we'll see if we can make the next edition even better:
Mike@Pacific-Coast-Highway-Travel.com

Made in the USA
San Bernardino, CA
17 August 2013